The Church

What is it? Who is it?

Chiara Lubich

The Church

What is it? Who is it?

Edited by
Brendan Leahy and Hubertus Blaumeiser

NCP

New City Press
Hyde Park, New York

Published in the United States by New City Press
202 Comforter Blvd., Hyde Park, NY 12538
www.newcitypress.com
©2019 New City Press (English Translation)

Cover design by Leandro De Leon
Layout by Miguel Tejerina

Originally published in Italian as *La Chiesa*
Copyright 2018 by Citta' Nuova Editrice, Rome, Italy.

Library of Congress Control Number: 2018963199

ISBN 978-1-56548-683-6 (paperback)
ISBN 978-1-56548-684-3 (e-book)

Contents

Series Preface*

"To those who follow you, leave only the gospel."

Chiara Lubich has articulated the gospel in many ways, which are outlined in twelve cornerstones: *God-love*, the *will of God*, the *Word of God*, *love of neighbor*, the *new commandment*, the *Eucharist*, the gift of *unity*, *Jesus crucified and forsaken*, *Mary*, the *Church-communion*, the *Holy Spirit, Jesus present among us*.

Since they emerged in the late 1940s, these points have been inscribed in the souls and in the lives of thousands of people from every corner of the earth. Nevertheless, since Chiara Lubich's death in 2008, what has been missing is a document that combined many texts, including those yet unpublished, that would illustrate them. This series of books seeks to deepen our understanding of these twelve cornerstones by presenting three sources from which they have emerged:

- the dimension of her personal testimony, especially as Chiara Lubich understood, deepened and lived these points;

- the theological dimension of reflecting on the mystery of God and of humankind;

- the dimension of incarnating these points in human life via a communitarian experience, in line with Vatican II (see Lumen Gentium 9).

---

* This volume contains Chiara Lubich's thought and experience on "the Holy Spirit." While it is the tenth in this series of titles originally published in Italian by Città Nuova, it is the fourth to be translated in its complete form and published by New City Press.

The series will include as many as twelve books, through which it is hoped that readers may discover:

- A great spiritual teacher who can accompany them in their spiritual life;

- A deeper appreciation of the communal aspect of Christian life, and the implications of a communitarian spirituality for the Church and humanity;

- A deeper and more personal understanding of Chiara Lubich's life and thought that they can apply in their everyday life.

Introduction

"What can we do to improve the Church?"

"It's very simple! We just have to start! It's up to you and me."

This short conversation between a journalist and Mother Teresa sums up what each of us can do in this time of challenge. Now, in a particular way, all churches, especially the Catholic Church, feel a strong need for a total renewal that begins by returning to our origins.

In today's global, multi-religious and multicultural society, characterized by increased mobility and mass migrations, with rapid developments in economics, politics, and the media, there is a growing sense that Christians need to renew their lives so as to make a real impact on society. It's not by chance that the ecumenical movement, which began a century ago, arose from a realization that Christianity needs to offer humanity a more united and more powerful witness to the message of Jesus.

A Love Story

In her way of viewing the Church and in her efforts to "be" the Church, through her charism of unity Chiara Lubich offered important ideas for living in this era of change. From the very beginning of her spiritual adventure, her approach was anything but passive. She encouraged an approach to Church that spoke of sharing in its life and generating it into life. She never considered it an institution outside or above the people. On the contrary, she discovered it (and brought many others to the same discovery) as a living reality, an event of communion, an interweaving of deeply personal relationships. In short, she discovered the Church, to use Pope Francis's words, to be a "love story." In this way, as a woman and a lay person, she made a significant contribution to a modern-day understanding of the Church.

This is evident already in her letters from the 1940s, when she was in her early twenties. When asked about the Church, her replies were clear: she was convinced that all the baptized are called to take personal responsibility for the Church, that the whole people of God has to be on the front lines. She contributed to bringing about this change of perspective by promoting a spirituality of communion and unity. She reached out to people of all ages and of every social condition and vocation, inviting them to commit to living a radically gospel-centered experience, and to do so not just as individuals, but all together, indeed, as "Church," *as a people.*

Many – One

After the initial years of the Focolare Movement,[1] when Chiara and her companions focused on living the gospel in a radical way, in 1949 they experienced a period of light and spiritual insights that was to be fundamental for this new community. Some of what they deeply understood in that period anticipated aspects of Christian life later highlighted by the Second Vatican Council. In particular, Chiara understood that participating, through Christ, in the life of God who is one and three, can bring many to live as one "soul." She un-

---

1. The Focolare Movement is considered to have been founded in 1943.

derstood that this is the deepest reality of the Church.

Of course, all of this corresponds clearly with biblical perspectives. It's enough to consider Acts 4: 32, "The whole group of those who believed were of one heart and soul." Or Paul's admonition for Christians to be "in agreement" and "of one mind" (1 Cor 1: 10; Phil 1: 27; 2: 2), urging them to have the same sentiments towards one another (Rom 12: 15-16; 1 Cor 12: 26).

We also find this idea of being one soul in some of the early theologians of the Church. For Origen and Ambrose, for example, Christian maturity is about becoming a "Church soul."[2] Likewise, as we can see in his rule and other texts, Augustine proposed the ideal of living with others in deep unity of soul. In later centuries, Thomas Aquinas spoke of the Church as "almost one mystical person."[3]

Perhaps focusing on the Church as "soul" might seem to be paying too much attention to a specific detail of it. But for Chiara, considering the Church as "soul" is not simply highlighting the Church's spiritual profile or its intimate unity, but rather is underlining what the people of God is called to be within society. We read in the anonymous "Letter to Diognetus," which dates back to the second century after Christ, "What the soul is in the body, so are Christians in the world."[4] Therefore, what emerges is the fact that the Church should not live for itself, but rather should act as a leaven in society, as a Church that "goes out," a Church with a very precise lay profile.

---

2. See Origen, *In Cant. hom.* 1, 10: *PG* 13, 46. See also Ambrose, *Exp. in Ps.* 118, 6, 8: *CSEL* 62, 112.

3. See *STh* III, 48, 2, ad1: "Caput et membra quasi una persona mystica."

4. *Epistle to Diognetus* 6, 1.

A Key Word: Charisms

Chiara Lubich's writings on the Church collected in this volume help us to reflect on an experience of Church that speaks of vitality and dynamic relationships. Her approach is clearly "charismatic," both in terms of the role attributed to the Holy Spirit in the lives of all believers, and also in terms of those particular gifts, called "charisms," that God has distributed to the Church throughout the course of the centuries, always in response to the specific needs of each era. In some cases, these charisms have an impact on the whole people of God. They direct the whole Church towards new goals or provide a new countenance to the Church in response to the needs of the time.

Certainly, the vision of the Church that Chiara proposes is far from spiritualistic. She underlines in practical, everyday terms what it means to be true sisters and brothers of one another, "sharing the same body and the same blood,"[5] to the point of a total communion of material and spiritual goods. She strongly underlines not only this, but also the need to remain anchored to the ecclesiastical ministers through whom Christ is present in the people of God as the "head" of the body. However, he is not present as one who "commands," but rather as one who generates and re-generates his "body," that is, all of us as "Church."

From the very beginning of the Focolare Movement in Trent, Chiara recognized the specific role of the apostolic charism in the Church. She saw a particular grace at work in the bishops especially, in "Peter," that is, in the pope, who has, as she affirms, the gift of "representing the Church in one person." In this

---

5. Cyril of Jerusalem, *Cat. myst.* 4, 3: *PG* 33, 1100

case, too, it was the Word of the gospel that guided her, "Whoever listens to you, listens to me" (Lk 10: 16). Yes, of course, ordained ministers have limitations – we all have limitations! – and yet Chiara always saw them, and taught others to see them, as instruments of the presence of Jesus, who guides and corrects, educates and animates, nourishes and supports his people. Indeed, with reference to Church authority, she speaks of the Church as "mother." And the Church is "mother" even, and in a particular way, when purifying us or putting us to the test.

We might ask: what would Chiara have made of the contemporary scandals and challenges facing the Church today? Clearly, Chiara had a gospel faith in the presence of Jesus in ordained ministers (and we can think here of this faith in the ordained charism that we find in great saints in the past. Julian of Norwich in her *Sixteen Showings*, repeatedly says that she "submits herself to Holy Church as a simple child should." And St. Francis is known to have had an attitude of obedience towards priests, even those who had mistresses, to the point of kissing the ground where they walked!). But Chiara was not blind to the scandals of the Church. She spoke of how painful situations in the Church seem to be like the crucified Christ of today who cries out: "My God, my God, why have you forsaken me?" (Mt 27: 46). Furthermore, she spoke of the mysterious, but real, sufferings of the contemporary Church as the stigmata of today's Christians. For her such sufferings weren't simply to be borne passively. Rather, out of love for Jesus Forsaken, we need to go out and take action, seek to repair injuries, heal wounds and build unity.

The Church in little cells

The model of Church that the charism of unity proposes is not in the form of a pyramid, the image that was prevalent for many centuries in the Catholic Church. Rather, Chiara proposed that the model of a "synod," a gathering of brothers and sisters who love one another. She envisioned the Church as living and journeying with Christ in our midst, as he promised, "For where two or three are gathered in my name, I am there among them" (Mt 18: 20). The risen Jesus is present wherever there is unconditional love (see Jn 13: 35; 15: 13), and therefore, the life and mission of the Church can be fulfilled through small groups of people throughout society, beginning with the fundamental cell of the family, the "domestic Church" as the early Church Fathers called it. Tertullian was convinced that "where three [are united], even if they are lay people, there is the Church."[6] This vision of Church is very much "people-centered," and is deeply mystical, while being fully immersed in society.

Thus Chiara indicates a way crucial to the task of evangelization as well as for what today is called "ecclesiogenesis," that is, the rebirth of the Church within every social and cultural context. Chiara drew inspiration from the gospel and from authentic Church tradition. According to the Church Fathers, Christians, as individuals and as a worldwide Church, are nourished and generated at two tables—the Word and the Eucharist.

Speaking about these two pillars which form the foundations of the people of God, Chiara does not refer so much to the proclamation of the Word or to

---

6. *De exhort. cast.* 7: *PL* 2, 971.

the faith with which it needs to be received, but aims rather at living the Word, at applying it to our everyday life. Likewise, with regard to the Eucharist, she does not center her thoughts on the actual celebration of the Eucharist or on sacramental communion, but on our *becoming* Eucharist, on *being* the "host" that nourishes others, on allowing ourselves to be "eaten," even by people who never go near a church. In this way, society can gradually be transformed.

Who is the Church?

The Marian profile of the Church is a theme that attracted Chiara. As understood by the theologian Hans Urs von Balthasar, from the very beginning of the Church, the Marian profile has always been alongside the Petrine profile. In our times, this Marian aspect of the Church has been highlighted by the popes, in particular by John Paul II. The spirituality of unity promotes values and attitudes in the life of the Church that reflect Mary in an exemplary manner, that is, in the desire for holiness, an intense faith, the constant practice of charity and an authentic Christian lifestyle.

In her writings, especially those from 1949-1950, Chiara develops this Marian theme, offering a vast panorama, since she sees Mary, the Church, and the whole of creation as intimately linked. It is said that the pope is "the whole Church in one person," and this can be said even more so with reference to Mary, in a dimension that can be called "cosmic."

In this respect, Chiara gives a stimulating answer to the question, "What is the Church?" She responds that it is not a "what" but a "who" because the Church is Jesus in the midst of his people. In St. Paul's words, the Church is Christ's "body," making him visible and allowing him to have an impact on humanity. The Church—to use a wonderful definition by the Lutheran theologian, Dietrich Bonhoeffer—is "Christ existing as community," and at the same time, is "Mary," that is, it is modelled on Mary.

In our contemporary world, many people ask, "What purpose does the Church serve? What does it do?" Chiara responds with a concept that is emerging more and more also in ecumenism, namely, that the Church has the task, within humanity, of being a catalyst for unity. And it can be this because it draws its life from God who is Love, from God whose life unfolds in three Persons—the Lover, the Beloved and Love itself.[7] Being three in one reveals to us that being "many" and being "diverse" is not detrimental to unity, but rather represents unity's intrinsic dynamism. Bringing this "trinitarian" leaven into every personal and social relationship injects a charge of love into them, thus renewing, transforming, and making fruitful every interaction. This is the great adventure that the Holy Spirit opens up before us today. Chiara Lubich's charism of unity and the experience of Church that comes from living it is a significant response to the challenges of this adventure.

Broad Vision of the People of God

In speaking of "Church," Chiara is not referring simply to the Catholic Church. It is true, of course, that she was born into a Catholic family, grew up and lived fully inserted in the Catholic Church, which she deeply loved. Yet very early on, members of the Lutheran

---

7. Augustine, *The Trinity* 8, 10, 14.

Church were attracted to her charism that is so deeply rooted in the gospel, seeing the Church as generated by the Word of God. Anglicans were attracted by the focus on unity, preserved through mutual love. The experience of Christ present in the community was of particular interest to members of the Reformed Church. For the Orthodox, the harmony between the Movement's spirituality and the theology of the Church Fathers was significant. It's not that the various ecclesiological issues that still divide the Christian Churches were resolved, but bridges have been built that help members of different Churches to grow in their understanding of one another, thereby facilitating a growth in unity, which views diversity as an enrichment.

Guided by the Holy Spirit and encouraged by the Second Vatican Council and Pope Paul VI's encyclical on dialogue, *Ecclesiam suam*, Chiara gradually developed a broad vision of the people of God, as wide as the universal embrace of Christ, crucified and forsaken, which includes every human being no matter what their situation. He is present as the risen Lord in the heart of every human reality[8]—often in ways we don't understand or fully grasp. On this basis it is possible to open a dialogue with all kinds of people, of every culture or background. Many have resonated with the Movement's experience and are motivated by it, even without sharing every aspect of its doctrinal basis.

In the Church and with the Church

We conclude our introduction with a quote of Chiara at a meeting held in Malta in 1999 which reveals her strong conviction. She stated: "Our life has mean-

---

8. See Pope Francis, *Evangelii gaudium* 275-280.

ing only in the Church, only within the Church . . . 'That they may all be one' (Jn 17: 21) was entrusted by Jesus to the Church . . . and our charism serves to reinforce this characteristic of the Church. Therefore, we need to journey through life with our soul in total unison with the Church."[9]

—Brendan Leahy and Hubertus Blaumeiser

9. Malta, February 25, 1999.

By Way of Introduction:
The Church as Mother

The following two texts offer an overview of Chiara Lubich's experience of the Church. The first, from 1950, summarizes the new life and discoveries she and her companions made in the early years of their spiritual adventure. The second comes from the mid-1990s, when she offered a retrospective glance at this experience while reflecting on the Church, one of the key points of the spirituality of unity.

We felt we were children of the Church

From the "Little Harmless Manifesto"

Trent, Italy, 1950

We found everything in the gospel. We nourished our soul on St. Paul and all the Letters. And all these words of God—as the Church interprets them—confirmed and inspired our way of acting.

"You have only one instructor" (Mt 23: 10). And Jesus among us was everything: teacher, father, guide. We didn't need anyone else in order to walk in the light, but we would not have wanted even him if the Church had not approved it. So, all the light that came from his presence among us was submitted to the one who directed us, since, as we had learned from the gospel, "Whoever listens to you, listens to me" (Lk 10: 16). For us there was no Christ without the Church and there was no Church without Christ. Jesus was the shepherd of our souls and, as the Movement expanded, the person who directed us was the shepherd of the diocese.

Even the light, although it was clear and overwhelming, was submitted to obedience, so that we came to understand more clearly that it was not the light that mattered, but the love for the Church, the humility that makes us recognize that we are children of the Church, subject to her teachings.

Perhaps because of this unconditional and total submission, we always had the feeling that the Holy Spirit who blew among us was the same Holy Spirit in our mother, the Church. One confirmed the other and vice versa: they were one.

It was beautiful to discover the Church as the seat of truth. Truth that emerged clear and new from within our soul where it lives (according to St. Augustine) was the fruit of our love for God. Yet, it was the same truth as the Church had been saying for twenty centuries and had held sacred as its own heritage.

Everything in the Church took on life for us. The dogmas, which had seemed stale and dead to our childish minds but that we respected and believed with blind faith, in the light of Jesus among us took on life, in the sense that, while remaining mysterious, they were no longer so impenetrable and inscrutable.

We participated in the light of Jesus, we were in some way in the Word, and the Word knows the Word. "For this reason I bow my knees before the Father . . . as you are being rooted and grounded in love. I pray that you may have the power to comprehend, with all the saints, what is the breadth and length and height and depth, and to know the love of Christ that surpasses knowledge, so that you may be filled with all the fullness of God" (Eph 3: 14-19). "You are the light of the world" (Mt 5: 14).

This knowledge engendered an ever-increasing love

for truth, and as a result for the Church and for Jesus. Everything in the Church took on life. We, baptized Catholic Christians, wishing to live the teachings of the gospel to the letter, submitted to the Church and, all united to one another, felt that we were truly Church, Church as "assembly." This is why we recognized ourselves to be her children.

And with what great ardor we went to her, to nourish ourselves with light. The sermons were illuminated by our love. Even the short and dry words of a poor preacher appeared to us beautiful and luminous because they were said by Jesus in the priest, and the doctrine was absorbed by our soul because they concerned the things most dear to us, those from above!

We understood and loved the sacraments as never before. And this is clear from the fact that, for the past six years (ever since the Movement started), all the people who adhere to it go to communion every day.

Unity cannot be understood without the sacrament of unity. He is the one who makes everybody one: one body.

I would like everyone to feel that they have a mother

From a talk on the main points of the spirituality of unity

8 December 1996

At the time when the Focolare began, the Church was often understood only as a stone structure, with Jesus in the tabernacle, and with statues of Mary, St. Anthony, or some other saint on the altar. For many people, the Church meant, in a certain sense, the catechism, first communion. . . It also meant the other sacraments, or festivals for some patron saint, or it might mean belonging to Catholic Action groups, and so on. "Church" meant the parish and the parish priest and, if people were aware of their existence, the bishop and the pope.

Through the charism of unity and all that goes with it, we understood that while the Church may be all of this, more than anything else, in the depths of its being, it is the people of God. We understood the Church as communion: the Church-communion.

Then the Second Vatican Council also defined the Church this way [as "communion"] and that caused a revolution.

What does it mean to live the Church as communion?

It means creating bonds of love among all those who are part of it, among its members, among its various sections (parishes, dioceses, movements, structures, councils, commissions, and so on). It means creating bonds of charity with other realities that are in some way linked to the Church (other Christian Churches, or other religions which are connected to the Church through the presence of the "seeds of the Word" in them, or in other cultures with their values).

Our spirituality teaches us how to practice all of these relationships.

It also means that persons in positions of responsibility create bonds of love with the faithful, so that love precedes each command (making those in charge people who "preside in love").

Moreover, the faithful should build bonds of love with those in positions of responsibility. This is documented by the following letters, which show that the Focolare's relationship with the Church was also marked by communion.

I wrote in 1969: "We did not act like this only out of obedience to the Church or simply for fear of being heretical! It was actually the Church drawing us to herself. Or better still, it was the Holy Spirit in us who urged us to be united with the Holy Spirit in the Church, because it was one and the same Holy Spirit."

The following sentence is from the early years of the Movement: "The focolarini[10] see the Church as a family in which, even though each member has to retain his or her own position and vocation, all should feel they are brothers and sisters, through love in Christ Jesus."

And everything is done in obedience to whoever has the charism of authority. In fact, we owe the Church an obedient love, a love that is then reciprocated, as we have always experienced.

We consistently had this attitude towards any bishop.

In 1960 I said: "I wish that everyone would feel that they have a mother, and that this mother is always there to nourish them. And I wish that everyone would seek out the authentic milk that is given by the pope and the bishops, drink of it and make it their own."

Thus one day a sort of hymn sprang from our hearts:

The Church, our most pure mother, has received
us into her family, opening to us the gates
of heaven, through her priests and the sacraments.

She has forged us as soldiers of Christ.

She has forgiven us and cancelled out our sins
seventy times seven.

---

10. "Focolarini" are consecrated members who live in community and take vows of poverty, chastity and obedience. They are men (focolarino for singular or focolarini for plural) and women (focolarina for singular and focolarine for plural).

She has nourished us with the body of Jesus. She has put a divine seal on the love of our fathers and mothers.

She has raised human beings like ourselves to the exalted dignity of the priesthood.

Finally, she will give us the last farewell; she will put us on our way to God. She will give us God.

If our hearts don't sing her praises, they are shrunken organs.

If our minds don't recognize and admire her, they are blind and dark.

If we don't speak of her, our words might as well dry up on our lips.

Only Unity Gives Witness to Christ

Chiara Lubich grew up in an environment in which the Church was a vibrant and multi-faceted part of life. Her native city of Trent in northern Italy was particularly blessed with many organizations and a variety of social projects. The Catholic Action groups involved most of the laity, both adults and young people, and the diocese had produced numerous priests, as well as men and women religious, many of whom were missionaries in various parts of the world.

Chiara was active in her local church and she benefited greatly from her contacts with the Franciscan community. She loved the fact that St. Francis of Assisi was "a revolutionary" and often drew on his spiritual experience for inspiration.

In April 1941, two years before the beginning of the Focolare Movement, Pope Pius XII named as the new Archbishop of Trent Carlo de Ferrari, who then played an important role in the emergence and development of the new Focolare community.

This was the context in which, from 1943 onwards, the charism of unity blossomed in Chiara as a "new way" in the Church, characterized by its communitarian lifestyle. In reading letters written by Chiara between 1943 and 1949 (a year that was to be particularly important for the new Movement), we note her continuous reference to the gospel, and her drive to unleash a Christian revolution in the world. It might surprise readers to notice how relatively rarely she explicitly mentions the Church. More than speak about it, she and her companions were living the vibrant experience of a Church that "goes forth." The relative silence about the Church itself was anything but a lack of love for the Church. Quite the contrary.

1. Living Members of the Church

The Church as family:
Everyone working for everyone else

When she was fifteen years old, Chiara enrolled in a Catholic Action group. A few years later, she was entrusted with looking after young women within Trent's chapter of Catholic Action. In the following letter to "the aspirants," it's striking to see the maturity of this nineteen-year-old young woman's adherence to the Church in its hierarchical dimension (with the focus typical of the time, that is, with the clergy at the center and the laity helping the hierarchy in the apostolate). It is noteworthy, however, that Chiara refers to the Church as "a family," in which the dynamics of communion brings "everyone to work for everyone else." Four years before the birth of the Focolare Movement (dated as 7 December 1943), we can see her great desire to give the Church a "soul" of love.

From a letter to young women aspiring to be members of Catholic Action

Trent, Italy, 18 August 1939

Dear aspirants,

Think of it, my children, what a gift the Lord has given us by allowing us to be born and live not as detached individuals, but all united in a family, from whom we receive help, comfort and strength in the various moments of our life.

Just as God gave us this grace in the natural order of things, he also gave us the grace, the gift of belonging to a much bigger family, in the spiritual order. He has allowed us to belong to the great family of the Church, from whom we received new life through baptism. We also receive, in the sacraments of the Church, the food and support we need to reach our goal.

In this family, the love of God for us is revealed through the love we receive from the head of the Church, the pope, from the leader of our diocese, the bishop, and from the one closest to us, who knows us personally, who knows and guides our soul, the parish priest.

In our own families, does our father work only for one of his children, or only for our mother or only for himself? And do the children work only for themselves or only for their father? No, of course not! Everyone works for all the others.

This is what happens in the Church, too. The good done by the saints and by the virgin Mary and the immense merits of Christ are all poured out on us and we spiritually enjoy them.

Everyone in this family, too, works for everyone else.

And this is due to the "communion of saints," a sublime truth in which we believe. . . .

Always stay united to one another. Pray for me. I always remember you!

To live for God alone

In 1946 Chiara wrote to two religious sisters who may have been praising her excessively. She attempted to show them that what is important is to direct one's whole life to Jesus and him alone. Her only desire was that her companions would have what she herself had: God alone.

These letters remind us that belonging to the Church means that we need to aim at holiness. Thus she calls all those who have consecrated their lives to God, as well as all those who have been baptized, to a radical choice of God alone.

From a letter to Sister Josefina and Sister Fidente

14 October 1946

My little sisters,

Since I love you in Jesus, allow me the full freedom of telling you the truth: "Cursed are those who trust in mere mortals!" (Jer 17: 5).

Your little sister, Chiara, might have so much love for you that it can't be contained by the whole world; she might, as you say, be inspired by the Holy Spirit; she might reach the highest level of holiness; she could promise her everlasting faithfulness to the friendship that binds us. . .But Chiara still remains a poor child, an imperfect human being, a paralytic when it comes to doing good, someone who ruins the Work of God.

How foolish is the person who trusts in another human being!

My little sisters, I know what you will answer. But *since I love you,* allow me to move you from your half-heartedness and throw you up into the heights, into the very heart of God.

"Blessed are those who trust in the Lord!" (Jer 17: 7).

God of my soul, my love, my all, speak to these two little hearts.

Speak to them with your divine voice.

Tell them that *you alone are everything* and that you live in them!

Tell them not to search for you outside of themselves, but to always find you in their hearts!

You know already, Jesus, how much I love them and always want to be with them. I, your spouse, would like to be with you in every heart that is in grace, so that I could make you loved! But I can't. I am and remain a human being. . . .

Speak to your spouses.

Tell them that one day Chiara could die, that they could lose any direct help from her, that human beings, precisely because they are human, are destined to pass away. Tell them that any person who trusts in another person merits a curse from you!

God alone is everything! . . .

My dear little sisters,

How much good your life can accomplish, being so similar to the life of Jesus when he lived and worked and loved in the little house in Nazareth!

But don't you realize that a person who loves in such a way that their life is *a continual life in two* (Jesus and the soul) does as much as if they were out preaching to the entire universe?

Now, stripped of your misery, which you will daily give to God, you are free to love,

And so—love!

He wants to live with you. And there's nothing he desires more than this *life in two,* life together with you.

It's only by keeping your individual souls closely united to Jesus that *the unity between the two of you* will be reinforced even more!

"Father . . . may they may be one in us . . . I in them and you in me, that they may be completely one" (Jn 17: 21, 23).

Only one idea: Unity

As well as drawing inspiration from her experience of living as "Church," Chiara also drew inspiration from the doctrine of the communion of saints.

From a letter to young people who were following Chiara

New Year's Day 1947

Keep one idea fixed in your head.

It was always a single idea that made great saints.

And our idea is this:

Unity

. . . Remain in the world so as to saturate it with the scent of lilies and to shout out with your lives that you trust in the one who conquered the world.

You know the world is cold and we, who want to give everything to the only one who has truly loved us in time and in eternity, should always keep our souls aflame with love.

Unity with your sisters [in the Ideal[11]] will provide you with strength and courage and help, because we believe in the communion of saints.

And when the coldness of the world threatens us, let's raise our gaze on high, where so many people have gone before us. Let's call on the saints and consume them in unity with us, so that we will remain faithful until death and receive the crown of life in heaven, where we all hope to be together forever, seeing, contemplating and loving Jesus, the only bond that joins us, whether we are near or far away.

2. Jesus in His Ministers

A central discovery Chiara and her companions made in the early times of the Focolare Movement was the importance of their relationship with the hierarchy of the Church. A great deal of correspondence took place from the 1940s onwards between Chiara and Archbishop Carlo de Ferrari. These letters are rich in historical and spiritual significance. They reveal a relationship that blossomed from the life of the gospel, as Chiara herself explains: "It was in reading the gospel that we understood and reflected on the need for, and also the beauty and joy of, being in unity with the Church authorities, as we lived the words, "Whoever listens to you listens to me." It was because of

11. The word "Ideal" refers to the divine gift of light found in the spirituality of unity, as well as to the new lifestyle that comes from living it.

this conviction that from the very beginning we entrusted ourselves wholeheartedly to our Archbishop in Trent. Our desire was to carry out always not only his commands, but also his desires."[12] *As some of the early commentaries on the Word of Life reveal, Chiara also recognized the presence of Jesus in priests, regardless—as she herself clarified—of their "possible defects." Hers was not a passive obedience. She had a powerful sense of the presence of Jesus in each person, as well as among those united by mutual love.*

---

12. Looking at the crisis in the Church today, especially the one caused by the abuse scandal, Chiara's attitude towards the Church might not be easily understood. It might even give the impression that Chiara puts her trust in human beings, while scripture clearly warns against that: "Cursed are those who trust in mere mortals" (Jer 17: 5).

Still her attitude is echoed by many of the great saints in the past. in her Showings, Julian of Norwich repeatedly says that she "submits herself to Holy Church as a simple child should." And St. Francis is known to have had an attitude of obedience towards priests, even those who had mistresses, to the point of kissing the ground where they walked. Surely, the crisis in the Church at St. Francis's time was not less than the one today.

For them, the Church, although a community of saints and sinners, is God's instrument for the announcement and the life of the gospel and of the kingdom of God, independently of how well each of us manages to live up to it. Ultimately it is the same Holy Spirit who operates through the Church and the scriptures, enlightening each one of us when we invite him in. And it is the same Spirit of Jesus whose presence we experience when through our mutual love, Jesus himself is among us.

It is this total trust in God that is being lived out by the great mystics and that brings about conversion among the people around them, including priests and bishops. And in this way are fulfilled the words of scripture: "We know that all things work together for good for those who love God, who are called according to his purpose" (Rom 8: 28).

Whoever listens to you listens to me (Lk 10: 16)

From the commentary to the Word of Life for the months of June and July 1947

We are taken up so much by the voices of the world that it is very good for our souls to listen to the voice of Christ—the voice of Christ!

. . . Don't expect Christ to come down on earth to talk to you.

When he was here, he appointed his ministers, those who would act in his name.

They are his priests.

Go to them with faith! . . .

Beware of this blind and deceiving world. Rise up to a purer vision of things. See in the priest the one who brings you the voice of Jesus, whoever he is, regardless of any possible defects he may have.

His word is word of God. That's what should be important for you. Don't stop at appearances.

Get rid of any discrimination or judgments that destroy the world, and live out your faith, which conquers the world!

The one who encourages and corrects us

A letter to Carlo de Ferrari, Archbishop of Trent

That they may all be one

Feast of St. Francis
4 October 1947

Your Grace,

I left the meeting with you with so much joy in my heart.

To understand my joy, Your Grace, it is enough that you consider just one fact.

I have spoken to many people, who also have a deep understanding of spiritual things, but I have never found anyone who understood our idea in all its clarity.

In you we not only found someone who understands us, but also takes the reins of our life so that we will walk in the way that the Lord has indicated to us.

You are really "our" bishop.

We thank God and St. Francis.

And today in honor of this great saint we promise you, with tripled good will, to be "the living expression of your desires."

Only in this way are we what Jesus wants us to be.

Since we are just at the beginning, prune us, correct us, shake us up if necessary, so that the Lord will not be deprived of the glory we are destined to give him.

We put ourselves in your hands, now and always.

Please give us your blessing.

The one who represents Jesus for us

A letter to Carlo de Ferrari, Archbishop of Trent

4 November 1947

You represent Jesus for us. You are our Jesus, the one who shows us "the way" and in the loving obedience to you, we find life.

Today, to make you happy, we promise you that the Word of Life of this month will be lived above all in our relationship with you.

In the conversations we were graced to have with you, we have tried to grasp your thoughts, your will,

and even your desires. We welcome every warning you
give us and transform it into life.

"I in you—you in me."

Like Jesus and the Father.

So are we with you.

We remain and will always remain in your will.
Your will is in us.

We want nothing else.

And "we in you" and "you in us" will bear great
fruit.

And these abundant fruits are what we wish for you
today, as well as for us, your "little sheep."

Bless us, Your Excellency, protect us, help us, use
us as you wish.

"All that is mine is yours " (Lk 15: 31).

3. Enclose Everyone in Unity

*The great desire that burned in Chiara's heart was to kin-
dle in others the fire of love for God and one's neighbor.
For this reason, she was strongly committed to serve in any
way she could to bring about the renewal of the Christian
community. She generated a wave of spiritual life that
eventually reached people in a wide variety of contexts—
from local parish communities to laity involved in various
fields of work, from communities of men and women religious to seminaries and houses of formation for priests and
religious. Her proposal was that everyone live mutual love
and unity so that Jesus' promise would be accomplished:*

"Where two or three are gathered in my name, I am there among them" (Mt 18: 20). It is a view of the Church that could radiate the light of the gospel in the world of today.

New horizons for society

From a letter to a group in the town of Anagni

Trent, 4 November 1948

My dear sisters in Anagni,

Since I'm writing to all of you, let me tell you something that's in my heart, which will certainly be useful to you.

It's God's will that all of Anagni fall into the furnace of the love of Jesus' heart.

For this purpose let's take advantage of every opportunity. May we accomplish to perfection the will of God that he asks of each one of us. Then, seeing our efforts and the partial results of our efforts to love (we're always limited!), Jesus, who is infinite, will open new horizons for us and give us totally new opportunities, launching us into every field of human endeavor, like fiery embers that will fill everything with fire. . . .

Don't tell me that the people from Anagni are tough, or that you don't have the skills or that you don't have time, and so forth. That's not true, because "Love conquers all!"

It's love that's lacking in our hearts! And too often we believe that loving God means offering hours of adoration, frequenting holy places, praying for long hours, and so on. Religion isn't only this, my sisters!

It's going out in search of the lost sheep, after taking care of the others! *It means making yourself all things to all people! Loving everyone who is near us as we love ourselves, loving them in practical and concrete ways, loving them strongly and gently. It's loving them as we love ourselves and desiring for them what we desire for ourselves.* It's being surrounded by a myriad of hearts that are awaiting from ours the word that gives life. It's loving, loving by denying ourselves, giving up *our own way of seeing things, our own way of doing things.*

The Lord is in urgent need of people like this: *people on fire!* People who are free of "spiritual problems," which are eternal obstacles to love! People who have burnt up everything, and long to burn everyone else in their fire. He needs people who are able to love each other with an open mind, who go beyond their own small circle and interests and get interested in all the interests of others—*before* their own.

He needs people who love each other so much that they submit everything to *Jesus among them* because they keep him alive through their ever-growing communion of spiritual and material goods. . . .

Jesus awaits these people who will be light and love for all those who are in the house. Bright, burning—candelabra!

Alongside beautiful churches let there be true Christians

The following letter was signed by Chiara and three of her first companions, Giosi, Graziella, and Livio. The context is the 1950 Holy Year.

From a letter to the Focolare community in Rome

17 June 1949

Next year will be the Holy Year. Oh, how I wish everyone would understand what I'm telling you! Rome will be the center of the world—people from all over the world will come here, the heart of Christendom. Oh! If only alongside the beautiful churches, the glorious monuments, the palaces and hotels, the pilgrims were to find, scattered here and there like flames, some true Christians, distinguishable from everyone else only because of their love for each other and for others, with open hearts like the heart of Jesus, ready to help everyone. They would leave everyone not only with the memory of past Christianity, but of a living Catholic religion, more alive and more beautiful and more interesting than the most beautiful monuments that are the treasures of Rome.

Only unity among brothers and sisters will give witness to Christ, the Son of God.

What I'm telling you could seem like a dream or just wishful thinking.

And so it is, for those who trust only in human beings. We, however, trust in Jesus among us when we are united, and so it will happen.

Already many people—lay people of every vocation, people in the international colleges of Rome and convents of sisters—feel our Ideal pulsating within them as the only hope. Jesus alone is life. If each one of us lives this fire, we will each ignite many, many other people and Rome will be covered everywhere in flames.

One Soul: The Gospel Incarnate

During the period called "Paradise '49,"[13] Chiara perceived divine realities in special illuminations, including a fuller understanding of the Church according to the plan of God. She experienced and discovered it above all as "unity." To be Church means to share in the life of God, who is one-and-three, living "trinitized" (to use an expression coined by Chiara) and to trinitize all of our surroundings. This leads to unity in diversity, accomplished in and through Jesus, bringing about the harmony of mutual giving and of accepting one another.

For Chiara, the Church is a reflection of Mary, who totally lived out the Word and who is the mother of Jesus, the Theotókos, *the mother of God.*

In this profound experience, Chiara felt very much linked to the whole people of God, whose central reference point is Peter, that is, the pope (and, as a consequence, the bishops).

At the same time, however, what stands out in Chiara is an awareness—at that time unusual—of the charismatic dimension of the Church evident in the wide variety of religious orders and, in recent years, also in the flourishing of many Movements.

It is within this overall vision that the Work of Mary— the official name given to the Focolare Movement when it was approved by the Catholic Church—has its own spe-

---

13. Note that capitalization in the texts from 1949 to 1951 is slightly different from the rest of the book [trans. note].

cific charism, which is "to unite all that can be united," to revive mutual love among all, and to give life everywhere to "living cells" of the mystical body.

It should be added that Chiara's understanding of "Church" went beyond the confines of the visible Church to include all humankind, because all, even though they might not be aware of it, have been redeemed by Jesus crucified and forsaken.

1. Many Who Are "One" in Jesus Christ

*In July 1949, Igino Giordani, a well-known Catholic writer and member of the Italian parliament, asked Chiara, whom he had met some months previously and whose spiritual pathway he wanted to follow, if he could make a vow of obedience to her. His idea was that they could become saints together as had happened in other cases in the history of spirituality. Chiara, however, felt she was called to "that they may **all** be one" and so she didn't want to take on a commitment of this kind between just the two of them. So she suggested to Giordani—whom she called "Foco"—that they should let Jesus in the Eucharist "make the pact of unity" on their nothingness of love, and thereby establish the bond that he desired for them. It was because of this pact, which in the following days her first companions also made, that Chiara and Foco found themselves identified with Jesus, as one soul, within the bosom of the Father. All who made that pact experienced that they were "one soul."*

In this way, Chiara and her companions experienced what the Acts of the Apostles affirmed of the early Christian community: "The whole group of those who believed were of one heart and soul" (Acts 4: 32). And likewise, they also lived out what St. Paul describes in his letter to the Galatians: "There is no longer Jew or Greek, there is no longer slave or free, there is no longer male and female; for all of you are one in Christ Jesus" (Gal 3: 28).

To be one and, at the same time, "trinitized"

In the following text, written several months after the pact of unity, Chiara is recounting what happened. She describes how the pact of unity helped her to experience, to understand more deeply and to live more fully the baptismal reality that finds its fulfilment in the Eucharist. Being engrafted onto Jesus makes us children of God in the one Son and brings us into the bosom of the Father. But it also unites us among ourselves, in a certain way like in the Trinity. In this passage, we touch on the most profound aspects of the Church.

8 December 1949

Before our entrance into Paradise we always spoke of the rays of the sun and we felt that each of us should walk along the ray of the divine will that lay before us, different for everyone and yet one, like the substance of the sun is one in the multiplicity of its rays.

And each of us felt his or herself clothed in light, the light of the ray, clothed in that one divine will that made us another Jesus.

We were Chiara-Jesus, Graziella-Jesus, Giosi-Jesus, and so on.

But when two of us, knowing ourselves to be nothing, had Jesus-Eucharist make a pact of *unity* upon our two souls, I recognized that I was Jesus. I felt the impossibility of communicating with Jesus in the tabernacle. I experienced the elation of being at the peak of the pyramid of all creation, as on the point of a pin; at the point where the two rays meet, where the two who are God (so to speak) make a pact of unity, trinitizing themselves where, having been made Son in the Son, it is impossible to communicate with anyone except the *Father*, as the Son communicates with him alone.

It is the point where what is created dies into the Uncreated, where nothingness is lost in the Bosom of the Father, where the Spirit says through our mouth: Abba-Father (Rom 8: 15; Gal 4: 6).

So our soul is the soul of Jesus.

It is no longer we who live; it is Christ, *truly*, who lives in us (Gal 2: 20).

The "three communions" as a basis for being one soul

In the following text, Chiara speaks of how the 1949 pact of unity helped her to experience the reality of being one soul in Christ with many others, which is, as we have seen, the most profound nature of the Church, and is also its vocation. We cannot attain this through our own efforts, but rather it is born and re-born from communion with Jesus, through living the Word, receiving the Eucharist and being in communion with him present in our neighbors.

In the meantime, we did not cease *living*, living with intensity, amid our tasks about the house, the reality that we were, living the Word of Life.

Every morning we received Communion, letting Jesus bring about what he desired, while in the evening at six o'clock in church, before the altar of the Madonna, which was to the right of the main altar, we meditated in a rather original fashion. I, thinking that Jesus wanted to communicate something of what he had brought about by the new Communion we had received, invited the focolarine and myself not to think of anything, to nullify every thought so that he could enlighten us.

In the fire of the Trinity we had been, in fact, so fused into one that I called our company of people "Soul." We were the Soul. Now the Lord, if he wished, could enlighten this Soul (through me because I was like its center) about the new realities and because of this it seemed necessary to us to have the maximum inner silence.

Then what I had understood I communicated to Foco and the focolarine. Our communions, therefore, were three: with Jesus-Eucharist, with his Word, and among us.

The Church-Soul: Spouse of the Word

After making this pact, Chiara and her companions lived an experience that Chiara described in terms of "Soul" and "Spouse of the Word". It parallels elements highlighted in the letters of St. Paul. On the one hand, St. Paul writes of the Church as the "body" that is born from Christ and represents him (1 Cor 12: 27). On the other hand, the Letter to the Ephesians speaks of the Church as the "bride" for whom Christ gave himself in order to make her resplendent "without a spot or wrinkle or anything of the kind, holy and without blemish" (Eph 5: 25-27).

8 December 1949

The *one* Soul, of the two of us and of the many united to us, and present in each of us—because united and if united—having arrived inside the Bosom of the Father, knew the Word and it was so.

It had the clear impression of being immersed in the sun. It saw sun everywhere: beneath, above, about, and it awaited new illuminations to accustom its eye to discern all who were living there.

It knew it was the Word, the expression of the Father within himself, and it understood it had been made Church in order to love him.

And so the Word wedded the Soul in mystical marriage.

The Soul saw itself as a little group of souls united in an infinite abyss of love.

To live the reality of the Church as the spouse of the Word becomes concrete in Chiara's experience, not only through communion with Jesus in the Eucharist, but in a particular way, also through communion with Jesus in the Word.

19 July 1949

Jesus from the tabernacle taught me how I should draw him to myself with love, almost breathing him into me, and how he was the Word of Life and how *living* the *Word* I would have loved him as Bride and he would have been me . . . *Living the Word in each instant.*

The Mystical Body: the canticle of the Trinity

In the following text, we see how being "Soul" and living the mystical body are intimately connected with the life of the Word. From this comes a dynamic that unfolds in ever new harmonies, so much so that Chiara calls this dynamic the "Canticle of the Trinity."

20 July 1949

In Heaven we will be solely Word of God and in the unity among our souls will be the harmony of the new song which is the gospel formed by the mystical body of Christ. Each one of us will be a Word, but, since each Word is the whole Word, each one of us will be the Word, will be a harmony = a unity. The new song is the harmony of harmonies! The song of the Trinity.

2. Unity with Those Who Represent the Church

No matter how luminous and powerful the mystical experience Chiara and her companions lived in the summer of 1949, Chiara always retained a strong sense that this experience blossomed within the garden of the Church. Therefore, it was always necessary to "lose" it in those who had the grace to represent the people of God as a whole. The model she took for this was the relationship between Jesus and Mary, a relationship in which Jesus clearly had precedence and yet it is nevertheless a "trinitarian relationship," that is, a relationship of reciprocity, as we can see in the account of the wedding feast of Cana (see Jn 2: 1-11). It also applied to the relationship between the new

Movement (the "Soul") and the Church authorities, identified here in the figure of "Peter," that is, the pope.

As Chiara explained some years later, this text also describes the relationship of reciprocity between the "Marian" profile of the Church and the "apostolic and Petrine" profile, between the Church's institutional-hierarchical dimension and its charismatic dimension.

In perfect peace

24 July 1949

I am in perfect peace . . . with regard to what the Church will decide about the future development of our Movement. . . .

Perfect charity casts out fear (1 Jn 4: 18) and I have no fear because I am Jesus; I am his bride entrusted to such a Spouse who, having given rise to this Movement, will maintain it by means of his Church.

Mary and Jesus in Cana

29 July 1949

When the Virgin said something to Jesus, she said it as she felt it, according to *the Holy Spirit* in her.

But Jesus—being perfect and not perfectible—making her renounce her will, her Holy Spirit, enlarged her capacity to acquire new Holy Spirit. And therefore he treated her with apparent harshness, because he loved her. . . .

She, obedient, submitted herself to the will of the Son, which was an enlargement of her heart, a loving more, and with this love of hers she (having been made

Jesus) was the Light of Jesus in such a way that he did Mary's will that had become his, that is, the Father's. Jesus, therefore, continually brought his Mother to the "greatness, perfection" of God the Father.

With her he never made *unity* of charity (as we say) *but of truth* and for her this was the perfect charity, for he did not adapt himself to her, but he adapted her to himself.

Perhaps now we can comprehend his words "O woman, what have you to do with me?" (Jn 2: 4). to mean "Remember that between me and you there is infinity . . . Therefore! enter into me and do with me the Father's will."

Then he performs the miracle requested.

Perhaps, as Jesus does to Mary, the Church (which is Jesus, the Holy Father) will speak to us, but we, obeying with our death, will illuminate the pope.

As Mary is with Jesus, so the "soul" is with Peter

29 July 1949

. . . But the pope (the true Peter) is at the head of all the Church, in the wider sense also of those Catholics outside unity (in our sense).[14]

Therefore, we, presenting ourselves to him, must die, that is, lose our (small) idea in his (big) one.

As Mary . . . submitted her idea to Jesus, enlarging it, so the Soul will submit its idea to the true Peter whereby it becomes idea of Peter, and that is *will of God*.

---

14. That is, those Catholics who do not know the charism of unity that the Holy Spirit has given to us.

The Pope: the Church in a single person

This excerpt refers in particular to the encyclical of Pope Pius XII, Mystici corporis, *published in 1943*

Rome, 3 October 1950

The pope is Jesus on earth, or better the Church in a single person. His words are *Life actualized*: they are words in the style of the Trinity where there is the ideal Light, Love that generates, the Father made actual. . . .

We are the Ideal (and the actualizing on a small scale . . . because the Son too is actualization) of this magnificent life on a large scale that is the Church.

I feel myself to be Church. . .

Rome, 26 September 1950

Therefore, I will follow the Mass with the prayer book and thank Jesus for not having had me do so except on rare occasions, given my precarious health, because only now does the Word correspond to reality: it is the Church that speaks like this and it is the Church in me that hears like this.

And I have a deep joy at having won such a gift . . . .

And it is also a prize from Jesus: I, just now, gave him the Movement because I lost it in the Church (the parish); he gives me the Church *and I feel myself to be so*. And this evening this conviction was so deep and rich and sweet in my soul that I was united with such intensity to the Church, was made to feel so much Church that I did not know if I was myself or if I was Church.

3. Charisms:
Christ Revealed throughout the Centuries

Among the writings of "Paradise '49" there is a text writ-
ten in 1950 that, unlike other pages, bears a title: "The
Church." It's a lengthy text and we can see in it the great
importance Chiara attributed to the charismatic dimen-
sion of the Church.

She opens up a vast perspective, saying that Jesus is
"the incarnate Word of God" and the Church is "the incar-
nate Gospel," or in other words, "Christ revealed through-
out the centuries." Just as the Word of God is expressed in
many words, so the Church throughout history has been
expressed in many and varied charisms, in charismatic
families, such as the religious orders and, in our days, in
new ecclesial movements and communities.

This variety, however, is an expression of their com-
mon origin, which is Jesus, the Word. In our times, it
seems that God wants to highlight this common origin and
the link that binds everyone together in the Church. With
her charism of unity, Chiara felt it was her mission to
contribute to fulfilling his desire.

The Church (1950)

Jesus is the Word of God incarnate.

The Church is the Gospel incarnate. Thus it is bride
of Christ.

Across the ages we see flourishing many Religious
Orders, as many of them as there are different inspirations. Each Order or Religious Family is the incarnation
of an "expression" of Jesus: a Word of his, an attitude of
his, a fact in his life, a pain he had, one part of him.

We see St. Francis and the Franciscans as the expression of the gospel Word: "Blessed are the poor in spirit, for..." (Mt 5: 3); St. Thérèse and her followers as the incarnation of the Word: "Unless you change..." (Mt 18: 3); the Sisters of Bethlehem, of Nazareth, of Bethany, and so on as concrete expressions of an attitude or a moment in the life of Jesus; the Stigmatines as the incarnation of Jesus' pain from his Sacred Wounds, and so on; St. Catherine, of the Blood of Christ; St. Margaret Mary Alacoque, of the Heart of Jesus, and so on.

In sum, we see the Church as a Christ unfurled throughout the ages. . . .

――――

The Church is a magnificent garden in which have flowered all the Words of God: Jesus, Word of God, has flowered in all the most varied manifestations. It is up to us to unite them.

As water is crystalized into tiny stars of every shape when it falls upon the earth as snow, so in Jesus, Love took on the Form par excellence, the Beauty of beauties ("the most beautiful of the sons of men").[15] In the Church, Love took on various forms and these are the Orders and the Religious Families. . . .

――――

The gospel that Jesus preached was the Good News, Love proclaimed.

Now after twenty centuries this Love has become concrete in the Church, which carries on the Incarnation and so has Christ for its head, and repeats the Incarnation and so has Christ for its Spouse.

---

15. See Ps. 45: 2 (but 45: 3 in the Italian version used by the author).

This is why the gospel preached at that time was Love.

The one preached now is Unity, that is, Love consummated: Love organized, so to speak, Love that has taken form and beauty in the Church: Trinity in unity.[16]

We have only to make Love circulate among the different Orders.

They must comprehend, understand, love one another as do the Persons of the Trinity. Among them, as the relationship that binds them, there is the Holy Spirit, because each one is expression of God, of Holy Spirit. . . .

———

Jesus is the Word.

The founders (heads of their small mystical Bodies)[17] are Words of life.

All these Words form the Church, another Christ or a Christ continued, the bride of Christ. It is the New Jerusalem, bedecked with all the virtues.

---

16. This means variety, multiplicity in unity: the various Orders united in the mystical body, the Church.

17. This is a way of speaking used throughout these pages and that is seen in other founders. It stands to reason that there is only one mystical body. Nonetheless, since founders are parents to their children (they have in some way given birth to them as, in his forsakenness, Jesus gave birth to the Church) and have transmitted to them their charisms (resembling somewhat Jesus who gave the Holy Spirit to the Church), what we have before us is a small body with a head—a body that is part of Christ's mystical body, and yet with the tint of the particular charism that God gave via its founder.

4. An Ecclesial Mysticism:
For the Life of the Mystical Body

As the experience of 1949 progressed, Chiara came to understand the reality of the Church much more deeply, as well as the specific mission of the Focolare Movement. In fact, it became progressively clear that it was called to be the "Work of Mary," that is, a body of persons in whom, in a certain way, Mary would be present with her life and her motherhood.

Just as Mary gave birth to Jesus and, at the foot of the cross, became the mother of his body, the Church, likewise the Work of Mary is called to contribute toward renewing and rendering more visible and tangible the reality of the mystical body. The way to do this is to live and to spread everywhere the spirituality of unity that increases the communion among all and gives life to an ecclesial mysticism.

An injection so that the Church
lives its divine life to the full

Rome, 3 October 1950

St. Thérèse brought something new into the Church. She put the gospel into light via a Word of life about which the Lord especially illuminated her. That Word has always been in the Church, but to St. Thérèse God reserved its "divine" interpretation in order, via the light's fullness radiating from it, to illuminate the Church.

We too have something new. It is new, this way of ours, even though ancient. Indeed, we found full of light the Word of Jesus' Testament: "Love *one another as* I have loved you" (Jn 13: 34), which corresponds to—and is amplified by—the Word spoken to the Father: "May they all be one ... I in them and you in me, so that they may be completely one" (Jn 17: 21,23), where the whole of the Church is seen as a mystical body whose Head is Jesus, by whom the divine, trinitarian, Life passes to the members.

We actualized it just as we understood it, and we saw it as the whole of the gospel in synthesis, a synthesis so complete as to have as its effect the best that one can hope: the fullness of the life of the Church, of the mystical body, where the members so live the life of Jesus as to be other Jesuses, not only through the life of grace that is in them and makes them participators in the divine life, but also because this life is so full and overflowing (despite being capable of having new fullness) as to be poured and poured out again upon our brothers and sisters, so as to make of all, through Jesus in the midst (who is "where two or more are..."), a single body, one soul, one Jesus.

————

. . . And our Ideal (I see it always more clearly) is nothing but a divine injection so that the mystical body, in other words the Church, lives with fullness its divine life. This is why the focolares were born, which in the unity of "two or more. . ." offer Jesus among the faithful in order to make the faithful all become other Jesuses, living and "healthy" members of the mystical body.

Ongoing creation of new cells of the mystical body of Christ

6 November 1949

Our Ideal does not only resolve human problems but brings a new theology, or better, gives a further development, perfects, completes theology and, in the process, ascetical discipline and mysticism.

The Church's doctrine is like a tree in blossom that has developed throughout the centuries. Our Ideal gives it a new blossoming: almost covering again the crown of this tree with an utterly new mantle of blossoms, and it seems—and it is—that the whole tree moves towards this blossoming, that it serves it, is for it. . . .

The peak of the spiritual life, before now, was the mystical union of the soul with the Trinity within itself by means of Jesus. Made part of his body, through him we were completely one with the Trinity. And perfection consisted in this intimate unending conversation of the soul with God. To achieve this: love for silence, for recollection, for solitude and, naturally, the flight from creatures so as to withdraw into one's inner cell.

It was the height of the perfection of the individual, who, united with God, let his Spirit flow in the soul and became another Christ. . . .

Souls in times past sought God within them.

They stood as if in a great garden in full bloom, looking upon and admiring a single flower. They looked upon it with love, both in its details and as a whole, but they did not gaze upon the others.

God asks us to look upon all the flowers because he is in all of them and only by gazing upon them all do we love more him than we do the single flowers.

God who is in me, who has shaped my soul, who rests there in Trinity (with the saints and the Angels), is also in the heart of my brothers and sisters.

It is not reasonable that I should love him in me alone. Were I to do so, my love would still have something personal, something egoistical: I would love God in me and not *God in God*, while this is perfection: *God in God* (for he is Unity and Trinity).

Therefore my cell, as souls intimate with God would call it and as we [would call it] my Heaven, is in me and, *just as* it is in me, it is in the soul of my brothers and sisters. And just as I love him in me, recollecting myself in this Heaven—when I am alone—I love him in my brother or my sister near me.

And so I will not love silence but the word (expressed or tacit), the communication, that is, of God in me with God in my brother or my sister. And if the two Heavens meet, there is a single Trinity, where the two are like Father and Son and between them is the Holy Spirit.

We should indeed always recollect ourselves also in the presence of a brother or a sister, but not avoiding the created person, rather recollecting him or her in our own Heaven and recollecting ourselves in the Heaven of the other.

And since this Trinity is in human bodies, Jesus is there: the God-Man.

And between the two is the unity where we are one but not alone. And here is the miracle of the Trinity and the beauty of God who is not alone because he is Love. . . .

Thus disappear darkness and unhappiness with aridity and all the bitter things, leaving behind only the full joy promised to the one who has lived Unity.

The cycle is complete and closed.

We must create continually these living cells of the mystical body of Christ—which are brothers and sisters united in his name—to give life to the whole body.

Bring love back into the Church

8 November 1950

The Lord has called me to found an Opera [=Work of God] that is a new wineskin in which is put the new wine (Mt 9: 17), that is, the new Spirit that he has given rise to on earth. From the wineskin it must be poured out upon the whole world.

God always does perfect things. For this reason, just as he made ready the humanity of Christ in the most pure womb of the Virgin Mary in perfect harmony with the Word who had to enlighten her, likewise he made ready a religious family, ours, in harmony with the Idea that it bears. It is completely one with the Idea. It is the Idea made life.

We bring back into the Church . . . the love that is God lived and we are thus in our small Opera like a small Church.[18] This is why there is room for both priests and laity.

We are a single Jesus . . . we are a unity, a simplicity, such that our life is utterly simple. It is concentrated down to just Holy Spirit. Like Jesus who acted under the inspiration of the Holy Spirit.

18. John Paul II to the Focolare Movement, Rocca di Papa, 19 August 1984.

And we are not afraid of speaking like this, because we are not afraid of God's gift, even the most delicate, when over all these inspirations there rules obedience to the Church.

5. The Church is Born and Re-born from Jesus Forsaken

Among the many things Chiara understood during "Paradise '49," one that is particularly important seems to be the realization that there is a link between the abandonment by the Father that Jesus experienced on the cross and the Church. It is precisely in the moment in which he no longer felt the bond with the Father that he transmitted it to us, pouring out on us the Holy Spirit. It was at that moment that the Church as his body was born and it is from that moment that the Church as communion and unity is always re-born. Chiara observes there is both a paternal and maternal aspect to this generative act of Jesus.

Christ is the seed of the tree, the mystical body is its crown

6 November 1949

Christ is the seed. The mystical body is the tree's crown.

Christ is the Father of the tree: never was he so much Father as during his forsakenness where he begot us as his children, in his forsakenness where he annihilated himself while remaining: *God*.

The Father is root to the Son. The Son is seed to his brothers and sisters.

Jesus Forsaken generates the Church

24 July 1949

Jesus who is Love would have wanted also to be feminine to be able to be himself: maternal Love.

In fact, he (apart from in his Mother) is mother *in the Church* (always bearing in mind the Church as many souls united in the name of Jesus and hence likewise Jesus).

But we can be Church (in this way) by passing through the mystery of the nothingness of ourselves, that is of Jesus Forsaken. (We became "Church" when on the nothingness of us [Jesus Forsaken] two who are Jesus-Eucharist made a pact of unity.) Hence Jesus Forsaken begot the Church.

The pangs of a divine birthing

25 July 1949

Jesus Forsaken is maternal love. His cry represents the pangs of a Divine Birthing of human beings as children of God.[19]

---

19. We understood why Jesus forsaken's expression was a cry. Like a mother crying out as she brings a child to the light, in the same way he cries out as he gives birth to human beings as children of God. . .

In that moment the Church was started, for in that moment there came forth from him the children of God.

In fact, in that moment he gave the Holy Spirit who was to come down—after the Ascension—upon the Apostles gathered together with our Heavenly Mother.

Within the People of God

For Chiara Lubich and the Focolare Movement the 1950s were years of light and darkness, of peaks and abysses, of pruning and abundant fruits. On the one hand, those years were characterized by a rapid expansion of the Movement with many new developments, but also by the pursuit of its proper juridical place in the Church. Because of this, the Holy See in Rome subjected Chiara, as its founder, to a prolonged investigation of her charism and of the new Movement. Chiara's attitude was that of placing herself totally at the service of the Church, considering herself and the Movement as a "child" of the Church, even when the Church, whom she saw as her "mother," severely tested her.

It was a decade full of challenges and trials, but one that was marked by extraordinary apostolic fruitfulness. We can see this in particular in the summer meetings in the Dolomite mountains, the "Mariapolis" gatherings, which continuously grew in numbers, with participants from all walks of life, who formed together a living portion of the people of God.

1. To Build the Church as a Family of Brothers and Sisters

The following text mirrors the experience of those years, which included a rapid spreading of the gospel life of mutual love in the Church and in society. The daily life of people was radically changed, resulting in a wide range of initiatives that influenced family life, the world of work, parishes and religious orders. The Movement soon spread from Italy to other parts of Europe and then to the other continents.

With the experience of "Paradise '49" as a light for their path, the life that had emerged as a "gospel revolution" in the 1940s continued. At the heart of it all were the focolare communities of men and women, at that time called the "Order of Mary." But around them there were also many other people who were living and bearing witness to its spirit. The "Work of Mary" was increasingly taking shape.

This text is entitled "How the Order of Mary relates to those who don't belong to it" and is part of a longer text known as "The 1951 Rule."

The Order of Mary does not live for itself, but for the Church

1950-1951

The Order of Mary does not live for itself.

Like Mary, who lived only for Jesus, the Order of Mary lives for the mystical body of Christ, the Church, and by loving it she finds her own holiness.

The law that the Order of Mary must live is the evangelical one of dying in order to live.

"No one has greater love than he who gives his life for his friends."

"He who loses his life will find it."

"Give and it will be given to you."

So, the Order of Mary finds its own development by seeking the development of the Church.

It is at the service of Jesus in the members of the mystical body of Christ.

It does not look for anything for itself but everything for others.

For example, it does not seek vocations because God will think of sending them if the Order of Mary will live for him in his Church.

It must therefore be in all respects forgetful of itself as Mary, and it finds this forgetfulness only by caring about others.

Focolarini live the Ideal of unity as "living hosts" to give it to those who do not have it. Wherever there is disunity, coldness, decadence, the cross, loneliness, sickness, war, quarrels, and so on they bring unity, warmth, heaven, companionship, health, peace, harmony.

Hence all the areas of the Church are an open field for the Order of Mary to act: the family, the office, government, schools, every human and religious society, convents of all the various spiritualities, associations and so on.

Everywhere, the focolarini, like "another Mary," want to serve Jesus; and to all, again like Mary, they want to bring Jesus: they have to bring Jesus because that is their task.

They help to revive the mystical body. They want everyone to feel like brothers and sisters, so that no one feels abandoned. They would like to help transform their religious and human environments into as many Paradises, where charity reigns and God lives among all. They want God's will to be done on earth as it is in heaven.

Around the focolares there is a large number of people who want to live the same Ideal, but will never be members of the Order of Mary because their different vocations do not allow it.

Between the focolarini and these people there is—by virtue of the Ideal itself—a fraternal relationship; Jesus, who lives among the focolarini united in his name, can and does live also among those who are outside the Order of Mary and absorbs everyone into one; he absorbs everyone into God, into Love.

Now in God all have their place and no one loses their own spirituality. On the contrary, it is reinforced because at the basis of each spirituality there is Jesus in whom all converge. Thus it is with the Franciscans, the Carmelites, the Trappists, the Jesuits, the Barnabites, the Servants of Mary, the Stigmatines; they are first of all Christians, which means followers of Jesus who said: "Love one another as I have loved you."

Omnes vos fratres estes. ["You are all brothers and sisters."]

And the mothers, the grandmothers, the virgins, the friends, the brides, the great, the little ones, the parliamentarians, the peasants, the priests, and so on—they feel they are in Jesus and for Jesus they feel they are all brothers and sisters.

The focolarini want to make this fraternity be felt by the greatest possible number of people and they foster it by serving Jesus in all their neighbors, whatever their vocation, sex, age or spirituality may be. They want to serve everyone, as Mary was serving Jesus, so that all may be one.

They do not want to bring any innovation other than the one of love in which they firmly believe, knowing that it is capable of changing the face of the earth.

Nor do they want to bring any new organization except the Order of Mary itself, because everything in the Church is already organized. Instead, they want to contribute to the life of all organizations, reviving in their members the love of Christ, so that all that is already done in the Church will be done with a charity that is stronger, deeper, and more continuous, so as to acquire a new value. . . .

They live in the Church as among brothers and sisters, they see the Church as a family, even though everyone needs to be in their own place, in their own vocation. Still, through the love in Jesus Christ, everyone needs to feel they are brothers and sisters.

Everything should be organized by love, since nothing is more organized than what is ordered by love, the love that leads to unity and so to the most perfect kind of society. . . .

They do not want to be a disturbance to any Work of God, but they want to help them all.

They love all the various vocations and admire them, because in all of them they find a particular beauty of Jesus who is the Way and in whom they would like everyone to walk together so as to break divisions, separations, parochialism and everything that is not catholic and so not universal.

In short, they want to serve the Church in order to serve Jesus, knowing that love is service.

Our Ideal and our rule does not want to bring any innovation other than that of love being placed at the basis of everything, with which—as we say of the Holy Spirit—the face of the earth will be renewed.

2. Beneath the Glance of Mother Church

As already mentioned, the period from the early 1950s until the first approval of the Focolare in 1962 were years of suspension. Not everyone appreciated the value of this new charism, even though it was producing many fruits. Accusations were levelled against it. It was a long and painful period during which the Movement was being investigated by Church authorities. In Chiara's words, "And so the night fell, terrible as can be understood only by those who have experienced it."

At several moments it seemed the Movement might be disbanded or that Chiara herself would be sent away from the Movement. During one of those moments, Chiara wrote to the men and women focolarini: "With this letter I want to say goodbye to you. Externally it's my last greeting to you as your mother. What I want to tell you is what Jesus told his disciples, 'My little children, love one another <u>as</u> I have loved you.' Always remain obedient to the Church, right to the point of death, death on the cross. Only in this way, in the unity among you and with the Church, will our Ideal invade the world—and it will be an invasion of love."

From 1952 onwards, the focolarine were in contact with the Co-Secretary of State at the Vatican, Bishop Giovanni Battista Montini [later Pope Paul VI]. In a letter to the Archbishop of Trent, Chiara commented, "You can feel in him [Bishop Montini] the love of the Church for us." In a previous letter she related that Bishop Montini had told her: "For you, being under the scrutiny of the Holy Office is a guarantee and a protection. The Holy Office is the Church, and the Church is your mother."

To be formed as "Church"

2000

Now, years later, we well understand that, if we had to pass through trials, like all others who commit themselves to a life of radical faith—and we even felt the need for trials—they should not be unlike the ones experienced by our leader, Jesus forsaken.

He had experienced forsakenness from the one he called Father, "Abba," whom he loved so much.

To us, these trials in one way or another had to come through whoever represents the Father here on earth, or our mother, that is, the Church, whom we loved so much, and in and for whom we wanted to spend our lives.

But just as Jesus ascended to the right hand of the Father after that trial, in which he had uttered his cry and became almost another Father, after our trial was over, we felt we had been made "Church."

And we were Church. We are Church. . . .

So in that period of time the only thing to do was to die, despite the fact that this painful suspension, so fertile for God's plans, was for some people an evident sign that the Movement was a Work of God. It was Bishop Giovanni Batista Montini of the Vatican Secretariat of State, [the future Pope Paul VI], who told us that to be under study by the Church was for us a protection and a guarantee.

Therefore, it was something positive, it was for our good.

No matter what happens. . .

From a letter to the Archbishop of Trent, Carlo De Ferrari

Rome, 5 January 1951

Your Grace,

It's true: the cross was heavy and it still is. And I understood Jesus "who fell" under the weight of the cross. However, Your Grace, I am happy, really happy.

And I received from Jesus the grace to be ready for every decision that the Church will make. . . .

I am happy, Your Grace, to be able to give to God all that he has done through me in the supernatural field. And I assure you that, whatever happens, you can be sure that I will always be faithful to my Jesus forsaken and very obedient to the Church. I reached this point because I never wanted to break unity with the Church, or better, with those who represented it for me. If I had not done so, this Work of God might not exist. But God gave me endurance to an incredible degree. . . .

You, Father, were a true Father to me and you showed me (something I only believed by faith) that the Church is our mother.

The caress of a mother

There would be much to relate regarding Chiara's relationship with Pope Pius XII, not least relating to the investigation undertaken by the Holy See. At the beginning of 1958, the approval of the Focolare Movement finally seemed to be imminent. But Pope Pius XII died before signing the papers and Chiara realized that difficult years lay ahead. She speaks about this in the following text, a note written the evening before Pope Pius died. Four days later she wrote to the focolarini: "It makes no difference to us to know what will happen to us. We know we are in the Church. We have always believed her to be our 'mother' and that's exactly what we have experienced her to be."

8 October 1958

The pope is dying. Or better, the pope is passing from this life to *Life*.

He was truly "our" pope. We know how much he loved us!

And maybe only now we realize how much we, too, love this pope.

Last Saturday he sent us a special blessing and we felt something out of the ordinary pour into our soul. I don't know how to say it, but it seemed that everything in the world acquired value; not only the big things, but also the small ones.

That unequivocal smile of the Church for us had the taste of a mother's kiss to her child.

Now he is leaving us and we have been heartbroken all day long.[20] . . .

---

20. This was particularly relevant because Pope Pius XII was just about to give official ecclesiastical approval to the Focolare Movement (Work of Mary) when he suddenly died. This meant that the whole process

But he is not dying, oh no! He will look on us from above, he'll protect us and help us!

Of course, this agony that we are living here together has given us the impression that, once he has died, also our Movement will have lost an enormous support.

In fact, for a moment it seemed so to us. . .

But no! God is the one who created this Movement and he will remain.

And the Church will also remain in these coming days when the pope may not be here. The real head of the Church is Jesus. . . .

Jesus, receive this soul who is coming to you. See how rich he is in talents, graces and merits. And up in heaven remember us, who remain here, still orphans, after having experienced how sweet is the caress of our mother, the caress of the Church!

Oh! What great desire to go there, too, now in these moments when night falls—but it's not yet our time! Help us to suffer, help us to endure this life, which in these hours seems so hard, so black, so devoid of any stars!

3. The Mariapolis: An Experience of Church

Within a few short years after the 1949 experience, a new reality called "Mariapolis" (City of Mary) developed and grew rapidly. Each summer people from all walks of life came to join Chiara and her companions to live an experi-

---

would need to begin again with the following pope.

ence of fraternity according to the universal values of the gospel. Although it began with only a few people, by 1959 this summer gathering had grown to number 12,000 "citizens." The Mariapolis then spread to many other parts of the world and soon permanent Mariapolises were established as "small towns" that witness to the gospel.

Many experienced the Mariapolis as a "Tabor" experience because of the powerful presence of God among those gathered together. Indeed, the Mariapolis was described as a "Church-city" where the "barriers between individuals and peoples are demolished, as well as all those divisions between the human and the divine, between the laity and the clergy, between society and the Church." Perhaps it's not by chance that this fruitful and novel experience emerged precisely in recent times, when the difficulties that face us demand a new choice of Jesus forsaken and a life of mutual love.

A living organism, "the mystical little town"

From a talk about the first Mariapolises

In 1951 our life together was given the name "city."

There was only one law for this living organism, and that was "charity," "love." Love was the only passport one needed to enter.

People could not come to observe. They had to build this mystical city, full of joy, together with others, where everyone competed to serve the others, and faced even enormous discomfort in order to be part of it.

1952 and 1953 were the years when a large number of priests and men and women religious from very diverse religious orders participated for the first time, and all their different spiritualities harmonized and shone out more brightly within the life of being one family. . . .

In 1955, the city received the name of "Mariapolis," city of Mary.

In 1956, there were representatives of every continent at the Mariapolis. We felt the need to keep in touch after we had departed, so that we could help one another to continue living the same way everywhere.

For that purpose, the magazine *Città Nuova* (New City) was inaugurated, as an expression of reciprocal charity. And due to this love for one another, editions were immediately published in the principal languages of the world.

In 1957, in addition to several persons with important roles in the Church, many bishops came to the Mariapolis. They said they felt the atmosphere of a living Church.

In 1958, taking our inspiration from a world exhibition of the best scientific and technical products, we wanted our Mariapolis to be a small "Expo of God," where spiritual values were highlighted.

And in 1959 the Mariapolis blossomed like a flower in full bloom. It was a model of the "city of Mary" that the "Work of Mary"[21] was destined to build up in the world.

People from twenty-seven countries were present, speaking nine different languages. United all together, they each consecrated their own countries to God, asking him to make all humanity the one "people of God." . . .

We often asked ourselves how the Mariapolis could have such a huge impact. . . .

The answer was in the life of Mary, since it was not so much she who shone out, but God who was present

---

21. The official name of the Focolare Movement, as approved by the Catholic Church in 1962.

in her heart. In the same way, the "good fragrance" of Christ, which the Mariapolis was spreading through-out the world, was not to be attributed to the fact that persons of the most diverse races, ages and social condi-tions were living together, but rather to God who lived within this Christian community, in which people lived constant mutual charity

Thanks to the Mariapolis, very many people came to believe in God, countless hearts began to love, and only heaven knows how many souls were brought back to life through God's mercy. All of this because people coming from so many different countries gave witness to God, people who have given him their hearts, so that among them the kingdom of heaven might shine out. . . .

Therefore, people from every walk of life arrived at the Mariapolis—married and single, men and women of every social class, laity and priests, rich and poor—and then left again in every direction, taking from the Mariapolis all that had entered their hearts, bringing about the most beautiful and varied vocations. The Mariapolis was the city set on the mountaintop that many had been able to see. What they learned from it and proclaimed was, "This is what the whole world should be like."

It seemed that it could be said of this splendid flow-er of the Church, which was born of and through and in the new commandment of Jesus, what St. Augustine had said of the Church:

> What Babel scattered
> the Church gathers;
> from one tongue came many;
> do not wonder:

this was done by pride.
Many tongues became one;
do not wonder:
this is done by love.[22]

People of God

*The 1958 Mariapolis was called an "Expo" of God, while
the 1959 Mariapolis was characterized by an experience
of the unity of peoples. New horizons opened up, well beyond the Mariapolis, prophetically pointing out the mission of the people of God for humanity today.*

Pope Pius XII said, "This is the era of the mystical
body."

Therefore, if we live this era well, its impact on society will soon be obvious.

One indication has to be that countries and whole
peoples will live in mutual esteem.

This will be something totally new. In fact, we are
used to having sturdy borders between one nation and
another, and to be in fear of the power of another country. At best we enter into alliances but all to our own
advantage. It is almost unthinkable to act solely for the
good of another nation, since the moral conviction of
the majority has never reached that height.

However, when life as a mystical body will be developed among individuals, who will really love their
neighbors as themselves, whether they be black or
white, red or yellow, it will be easy to repeat this law of
love also between one country and another.

Then something new will happen! Motivated by
love, which either finds, or makes, the other equal to

---

22. St. Augustine, Sermon 271

it, one people will learn what is best in the other and virtues will circulate to the enrichment of all.

Then there will truly be unity and diversity, and a new race of people will flourish in the world, people who are born from the earth but have been formed by heavenly laws and can truly be called "the people of God."

Passion for the Church

With the approval of the Movement by the Vatican in 1962, a new stage opened up for the Focolare Movement. The Second Vatican Council took place from 1962 to 1965. Chiara came into contact with key figures of the Council. Many visited the Movement's center in Rome. Others visited the recently founded small town in Loppiano in the hills near Florence. Often they commented, "But here the Council is being put into practice!" The Movement grew in and with the Church, with an ever increasing commitment to bring the spirit of unity into every aspect of church life. "Our one passion must be the Church," Chiara wrote in 1961 to a priest of the Movement. "We have to do what we can to make the Church more beautiful, renewed not through reforms we are incapable of doing, but through love, and therefore, by adhering to the will of God."

1. In the Wake of the Council

Chiara followed the Council with great interest. In studying the documents of the Council, she couldn't help but notice that focusing on unity and charity was the way to accomplish what they said. For her this was a call to con-

tribute toward achieving these goals through the life of the Movement.

A new Pentecost

From her diary

11 November 1965

I will mention it again here to further emphasize what the pope said last Wednesday, which is that we need to pray for the post-conciliar period, so that the bishops may have the strength and may find a good terrain in their priests and lay people in order to put into effect all that the Council has decreed.

Can we imagine what could happen?

In every diocese there would be an openness of love towards our brothers and sisters of other Christian Churches (and in places where they are not present, at least through fervent prayer). In every diocese there would be a more solid unity of priests with their bishops, reflecting the reality of episcopal collegiality. In every diocese a dialogue would begin with the world, which, if it feels loved, draws closer to the Church, and in every diocese all the other religions would develop good and productive relations with ours. In every diocese there would be increased fervor in the men and women religious. In every diocese the lay people would be launched into taking on their own responsibilities, each fulfilling their own human-divine tasks, which are not, and cannot be, those of the clergy, even though they should keep a watchful eye. Therefore, the "consecration of the world" would be a reality in and beyond the whole Catholic Church. In every diocese the people of God would receive an abundance of graces through a liturgy more relevant and more in conformity with the needs of the praying Church, whose members are united in the name of Christ. Just one Eucharist celebrated like that would be enough to convert who knows how many people!

And then . . . something that I don't know, but that I long to know . . . I want to nourish my soul and the souls of *everyone* in the Focolare with those holy decrees as soon as they are published. . . .

For this purpose, the Coordinating Council[23] is deciding that it will immediately begin a period of formation on the Conciliar documents for the various branches of the Movement, through our meetings in Rocca di Papa . . . until they become soul of our souls, blood in our veins.

While doing that, we will continue being formed in our own spirit, in accordance with the guidelines of our Movement, and in doing so, it will be as if the Holy Spirit descends on fire already ignited. Thus the Focolare will help to bring about that Pentecost which the pope pleaded for in his most recent address. Then we will be able to pass from "unity" to the "fire" that God and the pope want from us so as to set on fire a countless number of people. We have to reach the point of setting the world ablaze with a fire that will never be extinguished by any worldly water of any kind (and there are many!).

O Holy Spirit, make us become the living Church, through all that you have already suggested in the Council. This is our one and only desire. Everything else serves for this purpose alone.

---

23. The Coordinating Council is the central governing body in the Focolare Movement.

2. City Church

There are more than twenty Focolare "small towns" in various parts of the world, an expression of the gospel lived in the light of the charism of unity. The first of these, Loppiano, came to life during the Second Vatican Council and resonates closely with that great Council. Over the years, Chiara described Loppiano in various ways, not least in terms of its Church profile: "It was called 'Church-City' because it wants to be an expression of the most profound reality of the Church, that is, unity, the unity of hearts with God and among themselves. But it has this name also because it is open to dialogue with other Churches, with other religions and with the contemporary culture."

A living part of the post-conciliar Church

From an interview for a brochure entitled "A Day in Loppiano"

Loppiano came to life during the Second Vatican Council. This coincidence was certainly meaningful. . .

Certainly. The Holy Spirit acted in an overwhelming way in the Second Vatican Council. But the Holy Spirit is also present in the new movements, which arose at almost the same time as the Council and, like ours, were approved by the Church. And, if he is present, it's logical that he would highlight in them what he emphasized in the Council.

The Council affirmed, among many other things, that all Christians are called to holiness and that the whole Church is missionary. In fact, if you look at Loppiano, you can see in all its inhabitants the sincere, joyous, tenacious effort to reach holiness, and you can also admire their ardent zeal to bring Christ into to-day's world.

Vatican II restored the role of the laity in the Church. In Loppiano, where almost all the vocations of the Church are represented, it is beyond doubt that the majority of its inhabitants are lay people. There one can see how working for Christ is not only the concern of priests and men and women religious, but also of lay people, families and young people. . .

The Council emphasized the testimony that laity should give in the world through all that they do, for example, with their work. And in Loppiano work is very much in evidence and professional excellence is pursued with determination and perseverance.

The Second Vatican Council asks the laity to apply themselves diligently to the study of revealed truths and to insistently implore from the Lord the gift of wisdom (*Lumen Gentium* 35). In Loppiano they study and are kept up-to-date on various topics, so that they will be prepared to dialogue with the world. They strive to possess true wisdom that illuminates everything.

Vatican II states that "the laity should be particularly trained to establish dialogue with others, believers or non-believers, to proclaim the message of Christ to everyone" (*Apostolicam Actuositatem* 31). This is what all the inhabitants of Loppiano are being trained to do. And we could go on. . .

What, in your opinion, can Loppiano be, or become, for the Church and for the world?

It will increasingly become a living part of the post-conciliar Church, open to the world, in dialogue with other religions and with the main contemporary cultures to which many people can look to see the progressive development of the prayer of Jesus, "that they may all be one" (Jn 17: 21). It will increasingly become a city that will be a model for people today, of every race and nation, who dream of a united world and want to help build it.

3. The Profile of the Christian Today

The spirituality of unity gained new relevance in light of the Second Vatican Council. Since the charism unites the thrust towards holiness with a communitarian dimension of both the Church and society, it generated a Christian lifestyle that is both open and totally involved in the world.

A revolution to be carried out

In the face of the escalation of evil everywhere—in factories, schools, and neighborhoods—it is unthinkable for us to limit our Christianity to simply going to church on Sundays, and to being honest at home and at work.

The times we live in demand a personal commitment to be true apostles, in order to safeguard and reinforce Christianity, and to lead others to God. Contrary to those who are trying to snatch the world from God and God from the world, we have to give the world back to God, and God back to the world.

The revolution that the world is unknowingly awaiting *from us,* and which every Christian must carry out, is none other than an act of interior unification. Unfortunately, even when our life might seem to be good, in reality it is a continuous succession of acts that often become quite boring. It's a life with very little commitment, peaceful perhaps, but without much color or warmth. There is a time to work and a time to stop for coffee, a moment for catching the bus or for watching television, a time to sit down for the usual meal or a time to visit friends. Perhaps we even find time for church on Sundays and for doing a few good deeds.

But this kind of Christianity is no longer attractive for people today, since they can follow space ships into outer space, or experience new horizons opened by science, or, at least in their imagination, participate in important international meetings and decide the fates of nations and of the world.

This kind of Christianity has even less attraction for those who live for pleasure, who "seize the day" with no thought for the future, or those who dedicate themselves to the pursuit of art, whether genuine or otherwise. It also won't attract workers who, stirred by high ideals, struggle for social justice.

A total change is needed in the way most Christians live, a new conversion of heart.

Today we need to base our whole life on the words, "there is need of only one thing" (Lk 10: 42) and everything else will flow from that choice, as a fascinating consequence. This "one thing needed" is love for God. If we begin to love him passionately, if he takes his rightful place in our hearts and we adore him and serve him, then the lives of every individual and the whole of society will become imbued with his presence. Then, art and the apostolate, study and rest, family life and school, going for a walk or lying in a sick bed, will all become different verses of the one song, varied expressions of the one witness we have to offer to the world and that should be our only concern: to give witness to God. And then, also through us, he will come back "into fashion" in the world which, judging by the universal interest and attention given to the Second Vatican Council, is not so "worldly" as we might think.

4. Mind and Heart Opened onto the Whole Church

A constant theme in Chiara's life and writings is the ambition to spread love more and more at all levels of the Church and of society. For her, to be Christian meant to become holy not as an individual, by living a good and perfect life, but rather by having a Church-soul, by being Church, making one's own the joys and sufferings of others in the Church, as well as making one's own all the various dimensions of the Church.

What I love most

From her diary

9 November 1965

If God in his mercy were to call me to himself I would like to have a symbol carved on my tombstone: the dome of St. Peter's. For me that says everything. It speaks of what I love most and what I want to love most: the Church. Not only the Church with Pope

John or Paul VI or the popes who will come later, but the Church, the creation of Jesus, who died for it to be founded, his spouse now and in eternity.

To become holy as "Church"

From an article published in the Italian Focolare magazine, Città Nuova

25 September 1970

It is obvious that the way people considered holiness in the past is no longer understood or appreciated today, especially by the laity, and is even seen as outdated. People today want a style of reaching holiness that is beyond that of perfection sought as individuals. They often express it by saying, "We want to become holy together, we desire a collective sanctity . . . "

The countenance of the Church, with its areas of transparent light and also of clouds and shadows, should be reflected in every Christian, in every group of Christians. This means that we have to feel as our own not only the Church's joys, her hopes, the constant blossoming of new life, her victories. Above all, we should feel as our own all her pain, due to the lack of full unity among the Churches, or because of so many harmful disputes, or the risk that age-old treasures are undermined, or the anguish that so many people deny or refuse to accept the message God speaks to the world for its salvation.

In all these struggles, above all in the spiritual ones, the suffering Church seems to be like the crucified Christ of today who cries out: "My God, my God, why have you forsaken me?" (Mt 27: 46).

Not long ago I visited La Verna,[24] and while there I meditated on the exceptional gift of the stigmata that God gave St. Francis as a seal on his imitation of Christ, of his life as a Christian.

I was thinking that all true Christians should be stigmatics, not in an extraordinary, outward sense, but spiritually.

I seemed to understand that the stigmata of today's Christians are the mysterious, but real, sufferings of the contemporary Church.

If the love for Christ has not enlarged our hearts enough for us to feel the pain of these wounds, we are not what God calls us to be today.

In these times, becoming holy as an individual is not enough, and neither is aiming at sanctity as a community that is closed in on itself. We must feel within ourselves the sorrows and also the joys that Christ experiences today in his spouse, the Church.

We need to become holy "as Church."

On tiptoe

From an article published in the Italian Focolare magazine, Città Nuova

25 July 1970

If we feel joyful when announcing the kingdom of God to many people, who then come to swell the ranks of our Movement, but we are not equally joyful about the immense efforts and conquests that occur every-

---

24. The Sanctuary of La Verna, located in Tuscany, central Italy, is the place where St. Francis of Assisi received the "stigmata," a manifestation of the same wounds as the crucified Christ in hands, feet, and side.

where in the Church, then our charity is not perfect.

We should approach the persons that circumstances put next to us, trying to understand them, discovering in them, and in the groups to which they belong, the task, the mission, the plan God has for them. And to love these brothers and sisters of ours in such a way that God's program for them is accomplished.

Only if we act like this, with a love that wants the good and the development of other Catholic works as much as our own, are we worthy apostles, children of the Church who truly serve it well.

If we are called to participate in certain institutions that might seem outdated, before we decide to challenge them or to throw ourselves into a renewal, which might even be long overdue, it would be well worth it to place ourselves before God and consider the respect we owe to the Church and to all its members.

It is not Christian to stop only at observing defects or complaining about structures that seem to have been emptied of meaning.

We should remember, before everything else, how much suffering these works cost their founders. We should think of the faith, at times greatly tested, of the courage and sacrifice of their first companions, of the love the Church showed towards them at the time in studying them, supporting them, approving them, encouraging them. We cannot forget their past glory, nor the good, nor the fruits, often great, that they still bear.

These works must be entered "on tiptoe," as though we were entering a church, with veneration, knowing that our contribution is that of loving them—loving the persons involved, their goals, their activities—so that we rediscover together the beauty and uniqueness in them, and the value they have for today and that they cherish, to the consolation of those who are part of it.

Every work has its own function and is, therefore, in some way irreplaceable. The warmth of our love can help it to hear again the echo of the love of God that gave it birth, and it will have the courage to update itself, to increase and multiply.

As the sun cannot but warm, so love cannot but renew, bring new growth and rejuvenate every member and group of the mystical body, the Church.

Catherina of Siena, Church-soul

Catherine of Siena lived from 1347-1380 and was proclaimed a doctor of the Church in 1970 by Pope Paul VI. As well as being famous for her decisive role in bringing the pope back to Rome from Avignon, France, her life helps us to understand how to live with a Church-soul in every area of our life.

From an article published in the Italian Focolare magazine, Città Nuova

25 October 1970

Catherine was a person in whose heart charity burned so strongly that it was like Christ's. Hers was a love that became a true, holy passion for the Church.

Let's look at her in action.

Although she inspired a religious current, with many who followed her spirituality, which is summed up in the two words, "fire" and "blood," this was not her main work. Rather, her main work was her untiring effort to bring the pope back to Rome. Quite clearly in this task she was facing the problems of the Church with complete openness.

If we analyze her apostolate, we are struck by the same impression. At a certain moment, Catherine passed from a private to a public level. The immediate reason for this was the fact that among her followers there were also noted leaders and important persons in the political as well as in the religious field. But she saw all of them not through the distorted lens of one who has a restricted interest in a person, even though it could be a religious interest, but in terms of their whole personality. . . .

She shared with all her followers, who were her children, their struggles, their anxieties, everything they were living through.

She maintained a prolific correspondence, not only with men and women in the humblest circumstances, but also with Church and state authorities, and she was interested in news of current affairs, because of her openness to the whole Church and to all of humanity.

Then if we listen to her prayers, we have not the slightest doubt that she had only one great love. Her desires and her requests to God were for the Church. . . .

Catherine was restless until the Church would find its unity again around the pope. She lived and loved the Church so passionately that her every move was inspired by this flame.

Nor is the doctrinal side secondary in the virgin of Siena since she has been proclaimed a Doctor of the Church on account of her wisdom.

Catherine wrote books that Jesus himself dictated to her. And yet she was grateful to brother Raymond for all he did for her with his knowledge of doctrine.

He guaranteed that she remained faithful to the teaching of the Church.

Catherine acted like all true reformers. They submit their illuminations or revelations to those who can tell them the thought of the Church and let themselves be guided by those for whom they themselves are at times, in another way, the guide. . . .

Catherine was not scandalized and did not withdraw in the face of the disconcerting deviations of the Church at that time. . . .

Because the fire of Christ was burning in her heart, she experienced strongly the sense of the Church as a family. . . .

Not only was the Church her family, it was her home, her city.

Without doubt, everything that tore apart the net of relationships of peace, which should make the Church the city of light for the world, tore apart her own soul. . . .

As a "Church-soul," Catherine taught us that the Church is itself if it is *one* in faith and in love.

Today too, we need to learn from such a great teacher and our hearts will be inflamed by her ardent passion. Then we can all effectively serve the Church wherever we are on earth, whatever position of responsibility we hold, whether it be big or small.

Passion for the Church

From a talk to young people preparing for life in a Focolare community

Loppiano, Italy, 6 December 1966

The "passion for the Church" can be compared to a flame that liquefies a piece of metal of a certain shape and when it solidifies, it acquires a new form. This is what the flame lit in our heart by God should be. It should dissolve what is hard, impure, and deformed in us as individuals and in our group, and then forge each and every one into a different form. The original shape was the "old person," with a pre-conciliar spirit [before the Second Vatican Council], the form of the old society and the old humanity inside and outside of us. In the highest possible heat of charity, we will succeed in making our spirit melt and solidify into another form—the "new person," with the spirit of the post-conciliar Church and the form of a new society and a new humanity.

Forged and purified by this flame, the whole Movement will be able to contribute to implementing the vast reform begun by the Council, which will renew the Church, as only the fire of the Holy Spirit can do.

5. At the Service of the People of God

The passion for the Church and for the goals of the Church that Chiara felt so strongly became more concrete in the second half of the 1960s, with a series of initiatives and projects that touched on various aspects of life, ranging from youth to families and to society as a whole. In par-

ticular, she directed her attention to various aspects of Church life. Encouraged by comments made by Pope Paul VI on July 13, 1966, Chiara told a group of priests and men religious, adherents of the Focolare Movement: "The Council was celebrated in a spirit of community. Its desire was to give a greater sense of unity to the Church and to make charity circulate in more complete and concrete ways. Now you need to apply this spirit to the various areas of the Church you are involved in, that is, in your dioceses and in your religious orders." What came to life after that were a number of movements within the Focolare: the "Parish Movement" and the "Diocesan Movement," the "Movement for men religious" and the "Movement for women religious," the "Priests' Movement" and the "Gens Movement" for seminarians. A school of formation for priests also began at that time.

Love the Church

From her diary

16 October 1965

"Love the Church." This was the central theme of Pope Paul VI's talk on Wednesday at the public audience.

"Love the Church.". . . a word that goes to the very depth of our hearts. *For this, O Lord, we want to offer you our humble work during the few days of our life.* That is, to live for this Ideal, which means to love the ones Jesus loved, to love our Mother. It is love and the desire to be only love for the Church that urges us to work together with others to renew its countenance, by renewing our own lives every day and helping one another to be renewed, drinking at the fountain of beauty that the Church preserves and offers us.

It has to be this love for the Church that helps us invent totally new ways to show everyone . . . the miracle of its perennial youth.

The parish—the fundamental cell of the Church

In response to an invitation to priests on the part of Pope Paul VI during an audience on July 13, 1966, the "Parish Movement" began as a way for the charism of unity to serve the parish, the fundamental cell of the Church. Chiara commented: "In reality, if we manage to make parishes living communities, they will be like a light on the lampstand, radiating life in an unimaginable way." A further development came about in 1973 with the beginning of the "Diocesan Movement."

From a message to people involved in the "Parish Movement"

Rocca di Papa, Italy
18 June 1977

I have a very special wish for each one of you, both young and old, and especially for the priests.

My wish is that you may be in your parishes the salt and the light that raises the dough.

Yes, there will always be weeds. But this was foreseen by the gospel.

What's important is that all the good wheat may ripen and one day be gathered up by Jesus.

I would like to be one of you, to be able to put time and effort, and above all love and suffering, at the service of that splendid cell of the Church which is the parish!

But it's up to you! Here [in this meeting] you have been storing up a great deal of the ecclesial spirit of unity so that then each one of you can take it back into your own parish.

My wish for you is that the Christian revolution be born and unleashed with all its effects, such as the communion of goods, the conversion of atheists and of those living a bad lifestyle, the closest possible unity with the parish priest, who must never be alone in carrying out all his duties. In summary, my wish for you is that the kingdom of God may triumph in your parish as in that of the Curé of Ars [St. John Vianney], which attracted eighty thousand people for confession or, better, to conversion, to a radical change of life. . . .

Take Jesus in your midst everywhere. Nourish yourselves with the Eucharist. The "divine" will break through everywhere.

We are certain. Jesus said it, "I have conquered the world."

And he is still conquering it.

If I were a parish priest

On several occasions over the years, priests and seminarians asked Chiara what she would do if she were a pastor in a parish. Her advice was always to focus on the life of the gospel and to spread love among the parishioners so as to renew all the various dimensions of parish life. In this way, parishes would be projected outwards, working together towards the accomplishment of "that they all may be one." The following text comes from a response Chiara gave to the rector of a major seminary in Rome, who asked her, "How does Chiara Lubich view a dioc-esan priest?"

An answer given during a meeting at a seminary in Rome

22 May 2001

I would love to be a parish priest, because then I would have a particular area entrusted to me. In a parish, one can immediately spread the ideas and the spirituality of communion that the pope [John Paul II] proposes in his letter, "At the Beginning of the New Millennium" (*Novo millennio ineunte)*. This teaching could be communicated in homilies, in catechism lessons and in the school. The parish could become an example of unity for the whole Church. . . .

To put love at the basis for every task. The first Christians reached the ends of the earth because of the love that was spread by soldiers, merchants, mothers. . .

Today priests often fall into activism—and they destroy themselves, because they work and work, and then have no peace within, and so at times temptations can assail them, because they are alone. If, on the other hand, they live in communion with others, they experience the atmosphere of a supernatural family. Jesus is there, the risen Lord is there.

Charisms that shine out with new light

In contemplating the charismatic dimension of the Church which she had grasped more deeply especially in 1949-1950, Chiara offered some perspectives for the Focolare's movements for men and women religious.

From a talk to a group of men religious

1967

Your unity should not be anything organized. It has to be organized by the love and by the light of God, to the point of being a living contemplation. Therefore, what should the [men and women] religious do as the most important thing to be done? Live the spirituality. . . .

Give God in a charismatic form. But a charism that enlightens minds and warms hearts, in such a way as to draw others to God, with your life, with your faith, as perfect men and women religious who are united because they *are* "Church."

29 September 1974

The charism of unity sets in motion the sons and daughters of the founders, as the fruits of the various charisms, and helps them get to know one another, and unites them. Therefore, since charity gives light, everyone is then enlightened regarding their own vocation, which they feel within. Because if the men and women religious are the sons and daughters of a saint, there is the grace of kinship within them. They have the blood of St. Benedict within them, they have the blood of St. Francis within them. Charity makes this blood recirculate and they become more and more Benedictine, they become more and more Franciscan, they become more and more Dominican. . . And then we could say that they will start to resemble each other, because they have Jesus in common. It is Jesus who is at the basis of all Christian life, even before being the basis of religious life. At the same time, however, they are also distinct in their individual beauty, because the charisms that God poured out on earth are very different from one another.

A school of theology and spirituality for priests

In the autumn of 1966, together with Fr. Pasquale Fore-si[25] *and Fr. Silvano Cola,*[26] *Chiara established in Grottaferrata, Italy, what for many years was simply called "The Priests' School." Today it is called "A Center of the Spirituality of Communion for Diocesan Priests, Deacons and Seminarians," and is located in Loppiano, the Focolare's first international "small town" of witness near Florence, Italy. When this school for priests began, the Second Vatican Council had just concluded and was foremost in the minds of everyone. The following texts are extracts from Chiara's inaugural talk. In them Chiara asks if it is useful and opportune to promote an initiative of this type, desired by priests who had come to know the charism of unity. She goes on to outline some of the features that should characterize the school. In the years that followed, thousands of priests and seminarians have benefitted from this experience, which subsequently bore great fruit in their dioceses.*

From a talk at the inauguration of the school for priests

Grottaferrata, Italy, 24 October 1966

When the Movement was born, it was already in the mind of God that it contained within itself the

---

25. Pasquale Foresi (1929-2015) met Chiara during Christmas 1949 in Trent. He was the first focolarino to be ordained a priest (1954).
26. Silvano Cola (1928-2007) was one of the first diocesan priests to adhere to the spirituality of unity (1954).

seed from which one day a school for priests would be born, a spiritual school, but also a theological one. It is a school for priests who already know the Christian life and who already know theology. Is it, therefore, something necessary that we are doing?

In responding, Chiara cites a number of things that bishops coming from various countries had said. The bishops underlined the harmony between the teachings of the Council and the spirituality of unity, urging the Focolare Movement to give its contribution to the formation and accompaniment of priests. On this basis, Chiara then goes on to outline briefly some of the features that should characterize the school that is tasked with transmitting the spirituality of unity together with the theological perspectives of the Council.

What will happen if this school becomes a reality? . . .

It's inevitable that when Jesus is in the midst among priests . . . he will bring out the ecclesiastical priestly aspects that are characteristic of God's people! . . . While the Council nourishes all these things and casts fire upon fire, what needs to develop is a way to understand, for example, pastoral care in a new way, the liturgy in a new way, the seminary in a new way, and also a new way for priests to be kept updated or to do the apostolate . . . everything in a new way. . . .

We are laying here the first stone of something that is blossoming after the Council, almost as a fruit of the Council, even though its roots come from before the Council . . . and, as desired by the bishops, the Church will be imbued by this spirit through people . . . who have studied here. They will have studied not only the Church as it came from one particular Movement and, therefore, from below, but also how it has emerged beautiful and new from above, from the pope, from the bishops, from the Council. So, we too will give our contribution and will offer the world these new apostles, these new people.

A new generation of priests

After the Second Vatican Council, the Church went through a difficult period. On the one hand, there was the challenge of implementing in a balanced way the new avenues it had proposed. On the other hand, 1968 was the year of widespread student protests. This was soon followed by a crisis in vocations to the priesthood, with fewer candidates entering the seminaries. It was in this context that Chiara launched the Gens Movement (New Generation of Priests) an initiative for seminarians, which promoted a priestly lifestyle suited to our times. Chiara announced this initiative during a meeting in Loppiano.

27 April 1968

I would like to announce to you the birth of the Gens Movement[27] which has come to life almost unexpectedly. . . .

I must admit that its roots are deep and go back a long time, when many years ago, reading a book about the life of St. John Bosco, the desire came to me to one day offer the Church what John Bosco did in a time when there was a great shortage of priests. With his spirituality he formed dozens, hundreds of priests, who perhaps, despite having the vocation, would not have

---

27. Gens Movement: the new generation of seminarians inspired by the charism of unity.

become priests had they not been illuminated by the spirituality of John Bosco.

When I read this, which was one of the many services that John Bosco gave to the Church, a holy envy for this saint was born in my heart and I wished I could offer the Church a host of priests; maybe people who would never have become a priest if they had not met something that made them choose to do so. It is those wishes that God puts into our hearts that are then a seed that bears fruit years later. . . .

So, the Lord had to find a little alley, a way to bring to fruition this desire, which he probably had put in my heart. And now, here we are, on the feast of Easter, a movement has been born [the Gens Movement]. Three or four days ago, talking to Fr. Silvano, I told him that for some days now I felt inside me a drive—it was the Lord pushing me—to ensure that the Work of Mary also took care of young seminarians. . . . And I said to myself and to him that it would be a wonderful thing if the Lord gave rise to a host of "Gens" who, with the spirit of the Ideal of unity, would not only save their own vocation, but also remedy the fact that many seminaries, often in crisis, start with forty seminarians and end up with only four priests. Instead, if possible, they would begin with forty seminarians and end up with eighty priests, because in their seminary, unity would shine out so strongly that many other young men would be attracted [to the priesthood]!

6. For Unity and Fraternity

During the 1950s the Focolare Movement dedicated a great deal of its attention to non-believers. From the beginning of the 1960s, the ecumenical dialogue emerged, first with the Evangelical Lutherans in Germany, then with Anglicans and then with members of the Orthodox Churches. It was also during the 1960s that contact was made with Muslims. Increasingly these dialogues were seen as the specific goal of the Movement, very much in tune with the vision of Church outlined by Pope Paul VI in his first encyclical, Ecclesiam suam *and in line with the teachings of the Second Vatican Council (especially in the document on the Church,* Lumen gentium, *ns. 13-16). The following two texts refer to the theme of ecumenism.*

Passion for the unity of the Church

In 1967, Chiara travelled to Istanbul where she met the Ecumenical Patriarch, Athenagoras I, for the first time. A deep understanding was to develop between them.

Rocca di Papa, Italy, 2 July 1967

I would like to share with you a problem that I feel very much and that I brought back with me from Constantinople. It has become the passion of my soul.

It is about how to express what we call "our passion for the Church." In Constantinople . . . I felt the pain not so much of the passion of the historical Jesus of two thousand years ago, but of the mystical Jesus, of his Church, of the mystical body of Christ, of the whole of divided Christianity, that is all in pieces. We

Christians should work with all our heart and strength so that these divisions, these wounds are healed!

I would like to pass on to you, to each one of you, whether you are young, or live nearby or far away, coming from Italy or from other nations—we all are citizens of the world—to pass on to you this passion for the Church, so that it may become a reality. Of the 150 million Orthodox faithful, about fifty [million] are probably young people, and to whom do we entrust them, if not to you? You should pray for them! You should work everywhere for unity with them!

The solution to the problem of the unity of the Church is something we are preparing for today, and it will find its conclusion in the future! You know very well that the future is on your shoulders, not on the shoulders of the grown-ups! Who will finish what has started? Who will see the unity of the Church? Who will see the accomplishment of the last prayer of Jesus, "that they may all be one"? The Gen Movement[28] will see it! Therefore, you should take this passion with you from this gathering and ask for it every day in your prayers.

Accelerate the journey towards "That they may all be one"

The first ecumenical contacts the Focolare had were in Germany with a group of Evangelical Lutheran Christians. In 1968 this dialogue resulted in the foundation of the "Ecumenical Center of Life" in Ottmaring, not far from Augsburg. Over the years this center developed into

---

28. Gen Movement refers to the second generation of the Focolare Movement, youth from 18-30 years of age.

a small town where Evangelical Lutheran Christians and Catholics bear a common witness to the life of the gospel and mutual love. From early on, this ecumenical journey also had an impact on both Anglican and Orthodox Christians.

From a talk given at the inauguration of the ecumenical center in Ottmaring

23 June 1968

The unity between Catholics and Lutherans, to the degree this was possible, has been a formidable example, first for the Anglicans and then for the Orthodox. . . .

We have seen that this spirit of unity has some common ties with all these other Churches. For example, what is it that binds us particularly to the Lutherans? The passionate love of the gospel. And what is it that binds us to the Church of England? The desire for unity. And what binds us to the Orthodox Church? Love. Theirs is a mystical Church, and so charity, love [characterizes them]. . . .

What is our wish for this center at Ottmaring? That Jesus in our midst, who has led us this far, be always present here. And what will he do? Certainly great things, things we can't imagine. We see here a small center. It's like a seed, a mustard seed, but it's logical that if it is of divine origin, it will become a huge tree, because its destiny is an evangelical destiny, with the evangelical promises.

In this center we will try to increase the presence of God among us, of Christ in our midst. And how will we do that? By living the gospel.

Cardinal Bea always says that the more we live the gospel, the more we understand it; and the more we understand it, the more we want to live it.

So, if we Catholics and Lutherans live the gospel, what will happen? We will become more and more similar to each other and since everyone loves their own kind, we will love one another more and more. And, as you know, the gospel is not something static but very dynamic, and so it will make this little center a "city set on the mountaintop." And we are sure that many people will come to visit it and say: "Look at how they love one another and how they are ready to die for one another!". . .

And what will become of this small town, where everyone loves and Christ is in their midst? It will be a symbol of how Christianity should be today, inundated from all sides by the Holy Spirit. . . .

Charity is God among us, but God is not only charity, he is also truth. So we would like to offer our little center at Ottmaring as a meeting point for scholars of all the various Churches who serve the ecumenical cause from an intellectual, theological point of view. I am sure that charity, which is light, can greatly help the theological dialogue.

And we also hope that this center at Ottmaring, being both Catholic and Lutheran, can be a most suitable environment for our superiors, our bishops from both Churches, to come and visit and be welcomed by us, so that we can be of service to them in this way. . . .

It is a great joy for us that the passion for the Church that fills our hearts can be concretely expressed in offering this center to our respective hierarchies and scholars, as a place where Jesus' desire, "that they may all be one," can be more speedily accomplished.

A New Flowering on the Centuries-Old Tree

Canon Bernard Pawley (1911-1981) of the Church of England defined the Focolare Movement's spirituality of unity as a "spring of living water surging forth from the gospel." The mystical intuitions of 1949-1950, emerging after years of reading and practicing the Word of God, opened up a new window onto revelation. And yet Chiara saw the charism as nothing other than a flowering of the centuries-old tree of the Church. It is in this light that in the 1970s, helped by the studies of competent scholars, Chiara reflected on some of the key principles of the spirituality of unity in the light of the broad spiritual and theological tradition of the Church, particularly as expressed by the Church Fathers. In the course of these studies, charity and the presence of Christ among people (see Mt 18: 20) emerged as fundamental for the life of the Church itself. Other key points of the spirituality such as living the Word of God, the Eucharist, and unity with the hierarchy, were seen as a support for a life solidly anchored to those fundamental pillars, which were also the basis for the life of the first Christian communities from the very beginning (see Acts 2: 42). Unless otherwise indicated, these passages are from various talks Chiara gave to members of the Movement, collected in Scritti Spirituali, volumes 3 *and* 4.

1. The Church is Charity

The early Church's primary focus: to be charity

I just read a study on "Charity in the Second Vatican Council." I noted with joy how the Holy Spirit in the Council requires that the Church today re-model itself according to the spirit of the first Christians, in order to give the Church its true countenance.

For the early Christians, the primary reality of the Church was in fact to be *communion,* to be charity. All the other values of its structure are considered within this essential reality which gives them meaning.

Cyprian had a high sense of episcopal dignity, and yet he said to the clergy: "From the beginning of my episcopate, I made it a rule not to decide anything without your advice and the consent of the people."[29] As well as using the expression "common advice," "consensus," Cyprian uses other words like "co-presbyter," "co-bishops," "colleagues," to underline the communion among them. The important thing is this "being with" one another. . . .

The fact is that the Church, with Christ as its head, is the body of God, and God is charity. Tertullian affirms: "Where there are the three—the Father, the Son, the Holy Spirit—there is the Church, which is the body of the three." If this is so, if the Church is "organized charity," then what the Movement announces, in following its vocation, applies to the whole Church, "Above all, maintain constant love for one another" (1 Pt 4: 8).

---

29. Epist. 14, 4.

The entire Church, today too, and all of us Christians have to be, above all, full of charity.

All ecclesial relationships permeated by charity

Pope Paul VI strongly affirmed to the bishops of Oceania in Sydney: *"The Church is charity,* the Church is unity."

Previously in his talk he had explained, "The first communion, the first unity (in the Church) is that of faith."

Then he went on to say, "The second aspect of the Catholic communion is that of charity. You know what supreme importance charity has in the whole of the divine design of the Catholic religion, and what particular place charity has in the connecting fabric of ecclesial unity. We must practice in its ecclesial aspects, which the Council has emphasized, a more conscious and active charity. The People of God must accordingly be progressively educated in mutual love for each of its members; the whole community of the Church must by means of charity feel itself united within itself, undivided, living in solidarity and therefore distinct (See 1 Cor 1: 10; 12: 25-26; 2 Cor 6: 14-18). Hierarchical relationships, pastoral ones (as is well known), collegial relationships, those between different ministerial functions, social ones, domestic ones—all must have running through them an ever active stream of charity, having for its immediate effects service . . .and unity.

"The Church is charity; the Church is unity. This, it seems to us, is the principal virtue demanded of the Catholic Church at this moment of history."[30]

---

30. Paul VI to the episcopal conference, Sydney, 1 December 1970.

2. Jesus in the Midst:
The Church of the "Two or More"

Chiara was always mindful that the Church is not to be viewed simply as an "institution," but rather a reality to be lived out every day in a relationship of love with God and others. We see in sacred scripture that the people of God was characterized by the experience of the "God who is near" gathering his people into one. In the New Testament, for instance, Matthew's Gospel has its way of expressing this. In the Annunciation, Jesus is called "Emmanuel, the God who is with us" (see Mt 1: 23). The same Gospel closes with a promise, "And remember, I am with you always, to the end of the age" (Mt 28: 20). And then right at the heart of Matthew's Gospel we read Jesus' promise, "For where two or three are gathered in my name, I am there among them" (Mt 18: 20).

In reading the Church Fathers, Chiara appreciated more deeply the significance of this presence of Jesus. In its everyday life, both locally and universally, the Church is characterized by the presence of God in the midst of his people, the presence of Jesus among us! Wherever we live mutual love (see Jn 13: 34-35; 15: 12-13) this presence becomes palpable, is experienced by everyone and bears fruit. It gives witness to Christ even in places where external circumstances are not favorable to the presence and action of the Church.

To be ingrafted in Jesus, present in the Church

When the Focolare Movement first began, in the Catholic world there was not much talk about Jesus in the midst of people. The words of Jesus, "Where two or three are gathered together in my name, I am there among them," which we find in Matthew's Gospel, chapter 18, verse 20, were not particularly emphasized. . . .

From the very beginning, Jesus in the midst was everything for us—he was life.

Now that the Second Vatican Council has spoken about Jesus in the midst in such an explicit way, it has become something normal for many people.

But for my own and for all our consolation, I wanted to see if in the early Church this sentence of the gospel was given the importance we give it, owing, I think, to the presence of a charism.

When reading the Fathers of the Church, for example, I was astonished to see their line of thought in this regard, and through my contact with them, whom I can consider my Fathers, Jesus in the midst took on an even greater universality than I had previously felt in my soul.

Indeed, to explain the presence of God within the Church, which is of the greatest importance, since the Church without Christ in it would be nothing, the Fathers base their explanation on two sentences, "Where two or three are gathered together in my name, I am there among them" (Mt 18: 20) and "I am with you always, to the end of the age" (Mt 28: 20). Therefore, we are not referring to the simple practice, done out of habit, to which some people have reduced the life of Jesus in the midst, as when they agree about something. No, living with Jesus in the midst inserts us much more vitally into the presence of Jesus in his Church. . . .

We have always liked this sentence from Tertullian: "Where three are gathered together, even if they are lay people, there is the Church."[31]

---

31. De exhort. Cast. 7: PL 2, 971

Yes, because we are often a small group united and ingrafted juridically into the entire Church of Christ. Therefore, even if there are only a few of us, we are "Church," "living Church," because of the presence of Jesus among us.

Flying churches

From an answer to the citizens of the Loppiano

10 November 1975

What struck me most, in understanding better the reality of his presence among us, is that it's enough to have a few things for him: He says, "two or three. . ." and wherever he is, he creates the reality he came on earth to found—the Church. It is for this reason that he aroused within me an immense passion to build thousands and thousands of churches, hundreds of thousands, millions and millions of churches, not made of bricks, but of two or three people united in his name, scattered throughout the world. . . .

Won't this presence of Jesus in the midst in these "flying" churches, that can go all over the world, be "the soul" of the world of tomorrow? . . .

And all this can happen through small things, small just like Jesus born in a stable in Bethlehem, (it can happen) through two or more persons, who could be two or more boys, two or more girls, two or more women, a mother and a son, a daughter-in-law and a mother-in-law, two or more. . .

The family: a little church

By living mutual love with the measure of the gospel, it is possible to create and multiply living cells in the world, cells that animate, and renew from within, the Church and society. This applies in a special way to the world of the family, the small domestic church.

From a talk to the congress entitled, "The Family and Society: rooted in God so as to serve humanity today"

8 April 1989

Besides being the first cell of humanity created by God, the family has become the basic cell of the Church founded by his Son. Because of the supernatural love that permeates it through baptism and the other sacraments, especially through the sacrament of marriage, the members of the family are called individually and all together to the sublime and lofty task of making the family a small church, an *"ecclesiola."*

From a dialogue with families

In the couple we see two persons to each of whom Jesus addressed the following words: "Whoever comes to me and does not hate father and mother, wife and children, brothers and sisters, yes, and even life itself, cannot be my disciple" (Lk 14: 26). The couples [in our Movement] live—at least in a spiritual sense—the gospel in this aspect, too. They put God in the first place. In this way, their love is purified, sublimated, and becomes much stronger. Theirs is human love but it is also supernatural love, so that the presence of Christ can be established between them (see Mt 18: 20). And so the family becomes a small church. It is no longer closed in on itself. Around such a family there is always a wide range of activity, to the benefit of many, many people.

"Jesus in the midst" and the Council

According to the Church Fathers, both the Councils and their authority should be understood in the light of Jesus' promise, "For where two or three are gathered in my name, I am there among them." From what is said here, we can understand the many steps being taken in our day to imbue the Church always more with a spirit of synodality, that is, to walk along together, with the risen Lord among his people.

A great event, actually the greatest of all events, takes place every so often in the Church. I am referring to an "Ecumenical Council."

It is not of divine institution, but as Yves Congar writes, "Nevertheless, in the Council there is a certain structure, to which the Lord freely united his presence with a formal promise, "I am with you always, to the end of the age" (Mt 28: 20) and "where two or three are gathered together in my name, I am there among them" (Mt 18: 20). . . .

"In this we find a structure of the covenant (people meet together in the name of Jesus—Jesus becomes present in their midst) comparable on its own level with that other structure which is more of an institutional form, that is to say, more of a juridical form, the structure of the covenant constituted by the sacraments or by the hierarchical ministries.

"This is exactly how the Fathers of the Church understood it. . . . According to them, once these conditions have been fulfilled and these structures of the covenant are respected, in other words, once there is fraternal love and the fraternal meeting of two or three in his name, then the Lord carries out his promise, which is effectively bound up with these conditions,"[32] that is, he becomes present.

The Fathers tenaciously maintain that Jesus is present in the midst of bishops in the Councils. As a result the Council is like the great "focolare" of the Church where Jesus pours out his light abundantly, so as to enlighten the centuries to come.

3. The Word: Seed and Nourishment

In the Second Vatican Council's document on revelation we read: "The Church has always venerated the divine Scriptures just as she venerates the body of the Lord, since, especially in the sacred liturgy, she unceasingly receives and offers to the faithful the bread of life from the table both of God's word and of Christ's body" (Dei verbum 21). During 1974-75 Chiara offered the Movement talks on the topic of the Word of Life.

The Church feeds itself from two tables

The Fathers of the Church, who reflect the mentality of the early Church, often put the body of Christ and his Word on the same level.

---

32. *Orrizonti attuali della teolgogia* (Rome: Paoline, 1996), 172-73.

Clement of Alexandria pointed out that we must nourish ourselves on the seed of life contained in the Bible as we do on the Eucharist.[33]

"My refuge is the Gospel, which for me is like the flesh of Christ," says Ignatius the Martyr.

Jerome said: "We eat his flesh and drink his blood in the divine Eucharist and also in the reading of the Scriptures."[34] . . .

And Augustine had this to say: [35] "Tell me brothers, what do you think has greater value, the word of God or the body of Christ? If you want to answer in truth, you must agree that the word is not less than the body of Christ. Therefore, if when we are given the body of Christ we are very careful that nothing falls from our hands to the ground, in the same way we must be careful, when the word of God is given to us, not to let it slip away from our hearts, because we are speaking or thinking about something else."

The Church born from the Word

In the same way, St. Paul felt very strongly that he had become the father of his followers through the Word which he had sown in their hearts: "For though you might have ten thousand guardians in Christ, you do not have many fathers. Indeed, in Christ Jesus I became your father through the gospel" (1 Cor 4: 15).

Augustine saw the Church as born from the word of God: "The very apostles on whom the Church was founded, following Christ's example, preached the word of truth and gave birth to the churches."

---

33. PG 9, 10-30
34. Eccl. 3, 13
35. Sermon 300, 2-3

The Church, therefore, is born precisely through the proclamation of the Word.

In its turn the Church is a mother and gives life to souls through the gift of the Word and through baptism.

4. Jesus-Eucharist and the Church

St. Paul writes, "Because there is one bread, we who are many are one body, for we all partake of the one bread" (1 Cor 10: 17). It's a point taken up by many of the Church Fathers. Jesus, in the gift of himself in the Eucharist gives life to the Church and assures its unity both at the local level and throughout the whole world. In her talks on Jesus in the Eucharist in 1975-1976, Chiara reflected on this: "I once read that if the Church would not have had the Eucharist, it would not have been able to lift itself up towards God. Therefore, the Eucharist is considered to be the heart of the Church."

The Church as "one," called forth by the Eucharist

From a summary by Chiara of the main points of her talks on the Eucharist

The Eucharist does not only bear good and beautiful fruits of love and sanctity; nor is its primary purpose to increase our unity with God and with one another (as unity is commonly understood) and thus serving to nourish the presence of Jesus in our midst. Yes, this too.

But the task of the Eucharist is something else.

This is the purpose of the Eucharist: to make us God (by participation). By mixing our flesh with Christ's life-giving flesh, which is given life by the Holy Spirit, the Eucharist divinizes us in soul and body. Therefore, it makes us God. . . .

At the same time the Eucharist does not do this only for the individual person, but for many persons who, all being God, are not many, but one. They are God and they are all together in God. They are one with him, lost in him.

Now this reality, which the Eucharist brings about, is the Church.

What is the Church? It is the "one" called forth by the mutual love of Christians and by the Eucharist. The Church is made up of divinized people, made God, united to Christ who is God and to each other. If we wish to look at the whole thing from a rather human standpoint, that is, expressed in human terms, we can use an example from Scripture: the Church is a body, whose head is the glorious Christ.

The same body and blood

Here is what we find in Cyril of Jerusalem: "For in the figure of bread this body is given to you, and in the figure of wine this blood, that by partaking of the body and blood of Christ, you may become of one body and blood with him."[36] . . .

Cyril continues: "For when this body and blood become the tissue of our members, we become

---

36. Cat. Myst. 4, 3: PG 33, 1100

Christ-bearers and as the blessed Peter said "participants in the divine nature" (2 Pt 1: 4)."[37] . . .

In fact, in uniting Christians, through the Eucharist, to himself and to one another in a single body, which is his body, [Jesus] gives life to the Church in its deepest essence: the body of Christ, fellowship, unity, life, communion with God.

. . . John of Damascus writes: "[The Eucharist] is referred to as communion and it is an actual communion, because through it we have communion with Christ . . . and because of it we have communion and are united with one another. . . . We become members of one another, since we are one body with Christ."[38] . . .

Albert the Great emphasizes this reality in various passages: "Just as bread, which is the matter of this sacrament, is made one from many grains which transmit their entire content to one another and penetrate one another, so too the true body of Christ is made up of many drops of blood of human nature . . . mixed with one another; and so also the many faithful . . . united in affection and communicating with Christ the head, mystically make up the one body of Christ . . . and thus this sacrament leads us to hold in common all our goods, both temporal and spiritual."[39]

---

37. Ibid.
38. De Fide Orth. IV, 13; PG 94, 1154
39. Jo. 6, 64: B 24, 288.

5. Servants of All

In 1978 New City Press published Servants of All, *a collection of six talks given by Chiara on the theme of Jesus in the hierarchy. She reflects on the role of Peter and of the apostles, the role of the bishops and of the pope, and then offers considerations on the theme of "positions of power as a way to serve" and also on episcopal collegiality. She doesn't limit herself to doctrine, but explains how we can live in such a way as to unleash these "sources" that give us God, with all their graces. The book itself is well worth consulting. Here we will simply offer some comments made by Chiara on these topics on various occasions.*

Branches united to the vine

At a time when many were criticizing the pope and the bishops, Chiara invited young people to discover them as instruments of God.

Rocca di Papa, Italy, 9 July 1974

Another source from which we can draw to fill ourselves with God is unity with the hierarchy of the Church.

Today the Church is misunderstood. The pope is often criticized, the bishops are no longer seen as the successors of the apostles, and people no longer remember that Jesus said: "Whoever listens to you, listens to me, whoever rejects you, rejects me" (Lk 10: 16). . . .

Yet unity with our bishops has always been a fundamental point of our Ideal and a source from which so much divine life burst forth.

When we saw that some bishops, faced with the new ideas that came from our Movement, were apprehensive or hesitant about it, we were always ready to lose our ideas, even if we felt they came from God. Enlightened by our obedience, the bishops always changed their minds and asked us to continue along the way the Lord had shown to us. This happened many times. And I'm telling you this so that you will know what is behind the explosion of our Movement all over the world. We were like branches well united to the vine, and the divine life that God had placed in his Church flowed continuously from the vine to the branches.

The Gen have to inherit this faith in the Church and go against the current, against the negative current of our days that affects everything, destroys everything and extinguishes the divine wherever it is deposited.

It is clear what a Gen is. Like sunflowers that always turn toward the sun, the Gen always have to remain in front of those who represent God for us as if in front of God himself.

Jesus in the midst and the hierarchical Church

From talks given in 1975-76 on the presence of Jesus among those who are united in his name.

Who was it who always convinced us, beyond the slightest doubt, that everything we did was of value if it was done in unity with the Church, which is formed as a hierarchy? Who impressed on our hearts the certainty that the Church has always been a mother to us, and that as a consequence our lives had to be lived as children of this mother, even when someone who was not well-versed in the works of God might have doubted it? Who was it that gave value to Jesus in our midst, whom we tried to have present in all our meetings, if not the faith and the conviction that he was there in our midst because our little group was united to the whole Church and to all its pastors? Thinking back on it now, thinking of how young we were at that time, it makes my head spin. We could have erred a thousand times on this point, but we never did. The conclusion is that he who guided us to act like this was the Holy Spirit.

On this point, too, the Fathers of the Church powerfully confirm our line of action.

Cyprian says: "And let no one be deceived with an interpretation that empties these words of the Lord of their meaning, that is, 'Where two or three are gathered in my name, I am there among them.' He [Jesus] teaches us that we must always be firmly united together.

"Now, how is it possible for one to be in agreement with another if not in agreement with the whole body of the Church and with the entire community of brothers and sisters? . . .

"Therefore, when one of his precepts says: 'Where two or three are gathered in my name, I am there among them,' he who instituted and formed the Church does not divide people from the Church." [40]

From the same lips

Our modern age—like many other periods in history for a variety of reasons—is characterized by peo-

---

40. De Eccl. Unit. 12; PL 4, 524-525

ple who say they are nonbelievers or atheists, and yet they are attracted by Jesus and esteem him, even just as a man, and if for no other reason than that he was an exceptional person, out of the ordinary, someone who fascinates them. . . .

But our age, as we well know, is one that contradicts itself because [even though being attracted to Christ] at the same time people do not want to hear anything about the Church, which, as always, is the object of slander and persecution.

Yet the man who spoke those wonderful words, "Consider the lilies of the field…" (Mt 6: 28), and "Love one another…" (Jn 15: 17), and "Blessed are the pure in heart…" (Mt 5: 8), was the same man who later said, "You are Peter and on this rock I will build my Church" (Mt 16: 18) and "As the Father has sent me, so I send you" (Jn 20: 21).

Thus whoever thinks of Christ without his Church thinks of an imaginary person who never existed.

Perhaps such a delusion, which is quite widespread, is not altogether a bad thing. These admirers of Christ may one day really want to know him. If they seek him with trust and love and succeed in penetrating into his heart, they will find his spouse there—the Church, which was founded, loved and sustained by him and for which he gave his life.

The foundation stone

"And on this rock I will build my Church" (Mt 16: 18).

These words of Jesus are unequivocal. The rock upon which he is founding his Church is Peter, although elsewhere in the New Testament Jesus himself is called the rock and is certainly the stone rejected by the builders which became the cornerstone of the Church.

But Jesus was going to ascend to the right hand of the Father and had to choose someone else to be the Church's rock in his place. His choice was Peter. Jesus was not only the rock on which the Church was founded but was also the founder of the whole Church, which he referred to as a building. And so he chose Peter as the foundation stone. . . .

"Whatever you bind on earth will be bound in heaven; whatever you loose on earth will be loosed in heaven" (Mt 16: 19).

What a paradox! Therefore, heaven must be subject to Peter's decisions on earth. This can only be possible if it is Christ who lives in Peter. Heaven can only sanction what Christ himself would decree.

These words express beyond all doubt the divine presence of Christ in Peter, head of the college of apostles, the first hierarchy of the Church. . . .

Peter is an instrument of God and as such, God himself will act in him. But precisely because he is an instrument, Paul's words apply to him too: "But God chose what is foolish in the world to shame the wise; God chose what is weak in the world to shame the strong; God chose what is low and despised in the world, things that are not, to reduce to nothing things that are, so that no one might boast in the presence of God" (1 Cor. 1: 27-29).

In Peter one can see the common human weakness of instability. . . .

It is against this background of Peter's weakness, of his temperament with all its ups and downs, like in so many of us poor human beings, that Jesus' unchanging loyalty to the man he had chosen emerges with such majesty and compassion. It is described for us in John's Gospel: "When they had finished breakfast, Jesus said to Simon Peter, 'Simon son of John, do you love me more than these?' He said to him, 'Yes, Lord; you know that I love you.' Jesus said to him, 'Feed my lambs'" (Jn 21: 15-17). . . .

"That *more* (do you love me more?)," Pope Paul VI said, "demands . . . and brings about a primacy of love . . . . To the primacy of authority already conferred on Simon Peter, Jesus wants a corresponding primacy of charity . . . . He wants Peter to be the first in love for Christ, in order to be the first in governing the Church, that is, the first in loving the Church."

The one who loves the most

Here Chiara speaks about the experience of her first private audience with Pope Paul VI on October 31, 1964, which was similar to those she had later with Pope John Paul II.

In audiences with Pope Paul VI, I had, particularly the first time, the distinct impression of finding myself with a person who loved in a very special way.

The pope spoke with such wisdom that his words overcame all the juridical obstacles that were still in force. He understood and received in his soul the whole complex Movement that I was presenting to him. He encouraged me to tell him everything, because, as he said, "Here everything is possible."

I remember feeling that there was perfect harmony between what the pope said to me and what I felt came from God for the development of this Work. This impression was so strong that I almost believed that the room where the pope receives his guests had no ceiling and that heaven and earth had come together. If I had been brought blindfolded before that person without ever having heard his voice, I think that after a while I would have proclaimed, "I am with the pope."

Do you have a problem with the Church? Help solve it!

From an answer to a group of priests

Castel Gandolfo, Italy, 19 January 1991

The Church in our country has problems with the pope. How should we live this situation?

There are many situations in the Church, so many problems, and we can also contribute to finding the solutions to them. . . .

We should always have the attitude of being free children of God, even in front of Jesus in the bishops, and in front of Jesus in the pope. Then, with a lot of love, especially with concrete charity, we can express our difficulties, the difficulties we notice here and there, to the right and to the left. We give them, we offer them with love, so that the judgment made by Rome can be more objective, more perfect.

When we have done all our part, even if things don't go our way, and answers come that we don't like, we have to be at peace, we just have to obey, and that's all. . . .

We have to be the ones who keep alive the idea of the presence of Christ in the hierarchy of our Church. I am speaking now to Catholics, of course. . . . It is not a question of being progressive or conservative, it is a question of being people of the gospel.

We are not papists

From an answer given to a group of men and women focolarini in Brazil

There is a certain similarity between our charism of unity and the specific charism of the pope, which is precisely the charism of the unity of the Church. So there is a harmony between us, an understanding. . . .We feel this very much. But we are not papists, we are Christians, we follow Christ. Just as we follow the pope, we also love our brothers and sisters, and we love the bishops, always [with] this feeling of being children of the Church.

How the Church could be

Some time ago when I read a few lines written by Ignatius of Antioch, my heart jumped for joy. There I found words which could only have come from the Holy Spirit. There I discovered how the Church should be.

Writing to the community in Ephesus, he said: "It is proper for you to act in agreement with the mind of the bishop; and this you do. Certain it is that your presbytery [the counselling body around the bishop], which is a credit to its name, is a credit to God; for it harmonizes with the bishop as completely as the strings with a harp. This is why in the symphony of your concord and love, the praises of Jesus Christ are sung."[41] . . .

41. Ephes. 4, 1: PG 5, 648

Yes, the faithful, and in particular the presbyteral college [the council of priests], are to be united to the bishop as the strings are to the harp.

What does this mean? It means that, in his time, the people had a greater awareness of who a bishop is than people have now. Ignatius defined the bishop as he who presides "in place of God," in other words, God's representative. So, how should the faithful, full of this kind of faith, act towards the bishop? They should act as if they were dealing with Jesus Christ himself. They should open their hearts and minds to him, putting aside any personal interests in order to hear and accept what Jesus says through the bishop. Then the bishop, moved by Jesus and not finding any obstacles confronting him, but only love, can express himself fully, giving voice to the wisdom that uplifts, inspires and brings about great works.

Moreover, because of the unity of the faithful with their bishop, "like the strings of the harp," the presence of Jesus where two or more are gathered together in his name, would be manifest in a totally new way.

This presence would give greater meaning, fervor, brilliance, persuasion and strength to the bishop's words so as to make everyone more one in God. Through Christ's presence in the bishop and in their midst, everyone would "sing Jesus Christ," that is, Jesus would truly be reflected in a living Church.

Discovering the Marian Profile
of the Church

From the summer of 1949 onwards, Chiara realized deeply the link between Mary and the Church. Therefore, she particularly rejoiced when, at the end of the third session of the Council, Pope Paul VI proclaimed Mary as Mother of the Church.

With Pope John Paul II we see a further development. During a private audience with him on September 23, 1985, he referred to the theologian Hans Urs von Balthasar, explaining to Chiara the central role of the "Marian" profile in the Church, alongside the "Petrine" profile. In his Christmas message to the Roman Curia on December 22, 1987, Pope John Paul returned to this topic and mentioned it again in his Apostolic Letter, Mulieris dignitatem *(1988) in which he affirmed that the Church is "both 'Marian' and 'Petrine-apostolic'" and that the Marian profile "is as fundamental and characteristic—if not even more so—for the Church as the apostolic and Petrine profile, to which it is profoundly united" (n. 27, n. 55). This point is taken up in the* Catechism of the Catholic Church *(n. 773) and we find it also in the teachings of Popes Benedict XVI and Francis.*

From the 1980s onwards, we not only see this theme of the Marian profile in Chiara's writings[42] but she also

---

42. See Chiara Lubich, *Mary*, Brendan Leahy and Judith Povilus, eds. (London: New City, 2017), 115ff.

links it clearly to the charismatic dimension of the Church. For Chiara the Marian profile is expressed in the vitality of the gospel put into practice, in the charismatic thrust toward holiness, in the commitment to live mutual love and in the family-like spirit that should animate every aspect of church life. In this chapter we'll focus on just a few aspects: Mary and holiness, Mary and the role of charisms, the priesthood lived in the light of the Marian profile, the Marian profile and women.

1. Living Holiness Today

Léon Bloy wrote, "The only real sadness in life. . .is not to become a saint." Pope Francis refers to these words in his Apostolic Letter, Gaudete et exsultate, *34. Animated by a communitarian spirituality, Chiara always proposed holiness as a goal not to be reached simply in terms of the salvation of one's own soul, but as a commitment to live the gospel for the good of the Church and humanity. She indicated Mary as a model for what she called "a holiness of the people," lived in everyday life by loving God and one's neighbor.*

Inexhaustible springs

Learning from Mary, in her "school" as it were, means to strive for holiness in the midst of the world, at the service of others. Our commitment to do this is reinforced by the example of the saints.

From a text written before 1963

We need to live our lives today, or rather, it would be simpler to say, we need to aim at holiness today, bearing in mind that our style of holiness has to flourish in the flowerbed of the Church, where a thousand fragrances already spread their perfume.

We must harmonize ours with these, or better, find the true nature and fullness of ours in harmony with all the others. The scriptures, tradition and the sacred history of humanity up to this day have produced inexhaustible springs of holiness. Therefore, if we want to know well how to do meditation, we should seek out the contemplative saints to whom God gave priceless charisms. And, if we want to do the spiritual exercises, we cannot ignore St. Ignatius who is the master in that. Likewise, St. Francis will always teach everyone what true poverty is and St. Thérèse of Lisieux will give advice to those who want to reach holiness in a short time. Giving value to the saints is to glorify God in them.

A unique experience

From her diary

17 July 1970

I went to Subiaco[43] to go to confession. I was not able to tour the abbey. There wasn't time.

I had hardly entered when I was deeply touched by the charity of the doorkeeper—a little brother, old and lame, who escorted me into the church.

In confession, however, I had a unique experience. I was touched from the very first words that holy monk said.

---

43. Benedictine abbey in central Italy, site of St. Benedict's first monastery.

It is difficult to explain what happened, and yet I can say it in a few words—I met God.

It seemed that from the soul of that priest gushed a spring that had its origins sixteen centuries ago in Benedict and went back to the pierced side of Christ the Savior.

I wanted to stay in that church for ever, taken up by that deep emotion.

I envied that austere life that had openly and decisively broken with the world.

Now I understand why the abbeys survive throughout the centuries and are eternally modern. It's because people live there who already dwell in heaven and they communicate that atmosphere to you sweetly, so that it completely penetrates you.

I saw our Christian life, in contrast, as being very difficult. We are always in contact with a world devoid of God, always with occasions for compromise, because we are frightened, sometimes, of the hatred that will come to us.

Only a strong decision to live within, totally projected in the will of God of the present moment, will give us the hope that we, too, can be bearers of God, and not just of words.

One monk is worth more than a community of a thousand good persons who are not in perfect unity, who are not full of the fire of love for God and neighbor.

Saint Benedict can be satisfied.

Now that I have found living gold in the Benedictines of Subiaco, one day, if God wills, I will also visit the monastery and its walls that are witnesses of such holiness.

2. The Charismatic and Hierarchical Dimensions of the Church

Speaking at a meeting for religious in February 1979, Chiara commented, "I think we can say that charisms have a lot to do with Mary because she is full of charisms." And she went on to refer to Mary as "charism personified." All the charisms in the Church, she noted, are contained in Mary.

At the same time, Chiara was always attentive to the relationship of reciprocity between the charismatic and hierarchical dimensions of the Church. It is no surprise, therefore, that she was overjoyed when, at the meeting of Movements on the vigil of Pentecost 1998, Pope John Paul II spoke of charism and hierarchy as "co-essential." The recent letter issued by the Congregation for the Doctrine of the Faith, Iuvenescit ecclesia, further reflects on this relationship. Drawing on Hans Urs von Balthasar and on her experience of 1949, Chiara spoke of her personal experience of the interaction between the Marian and Petrine profiles of the Church.

The hierarchy and the charism complement one another

From an article on "The Holy Spirit and the charisms"

March – April 1984

It is believed, at times, and has often been believed throughout the centuries, that there is a conflict between the hierarchy of the Church, governed by the pope and the bishops, and the charismatic Church, animated by particular gifts of the Holy Spirit.

In reality, it is not like that. The Church, seen in the aspect of its hierarchy, and the Church admired because of particular charisms are complementary aspects of the one Church.

Christ founded his Church on the apostles and on the prophets (see Eph 2: 20). He did not conceive of a Church that was only hierarchical nor one that was only charismatic. Rather, hierarchy and charisms are the work of the same Spirit, of the one Spirit, the Holy Spirit, who gave life to the one Church.

Naming the various charisms, Paul begins: "God has appointed in the Church first apostles, second prophets. . ." (1 Cor 12: 28). This is like saying, for the centuries to come, some are appointed by God in the first place to be popes and bishops, and in the second place to be a variety of charismatic persons.

Using a closely approximate comparison, we can say that conceiving the Church without the charism of the apostles would be like conceiving a tree almost exclusively with only leaves, flowers and fruits, without trunk and branches. [On the other hand] conceiving the Church with only the apostles would be like imagining a tree almost exclusively with trunk and branches.

Both the hierarchy and the prophets serve the Church, but although they express their service in a different way, they are both inspired by the Holy Spirit and endowed with charisms to build up the Church.

The charism of the hierarchy, which the Holy Spirit gives in an orderly way through apostolic succession, serves more to guide, instruct and sanctify the Church. The charisms of the prophets are also bestowed by the Holy Spirit, who blows where he wills, and when it seems useful to him, with divine loving fantasy, he pours them out in order to renew, embellish, and fortify the Church as the bride of Christ. The Church shines more as bride of Christ because of these charisms of the prophets.

Just as Jesus, by the work of the Holy Spirit, is the Word of God made flesh, so the Church, by the work of the Holy Spirit in these extraordinary gifts, is more noticeably the Gospel incarnate.

The Marian profile of the Church and the ecclesial movements

From a lecture given at St. Mary's College, Twickenham

London, 16 June 2004

These movements came into great evidence in the Catholic Church on the vigil of Pentecost, 1998. St. Peter's Square in Rome, as well as the nearby streets and squares, were crowded with three to four hundred thousand people. They had gathered around John Paul II who wished to entrust to them, to those who were following the event on radio or television, and to history, an absolutely unexpected announcement: his vision of the Church today.

He affirmed that just as there is the institutional, hierarchical aspect of the Church, which is very important and essential, essential too is the charismatic aspect of the Church which is in profound communion with the first. This latter aspect is the effect of the various charisms given by the Holy Spirit to the Church, his spouse, down through the centuries and which are present now too in the new movements and ecclesial communities.

In this way the pope assigned to us, participants from more than sixty ecclesial movements present on that day, our place in the Church. We were—this is what he said—"a significant expression" of the charismatic aspect of the Church, although not the only one.[44]

The joy that filled our hearts on that day was indeed immense.

In view of this event, we can ask ourselves: who prompted the pope to speak in this way? Undoubtedly it was the Holy Spirit. Nevertheless, knowing his great devotion to the mother of God and the bond that she, who is filled with charisms, has with all that concerns these gifts, we have to think that he was prompted to do so also by Mary. . . .

Hans Urs von Balthasar, the well-known and distinguished Swiss theologian wrote in depth about the Marian profile. He affirmed that in the bride of Christ there are two distinct profiles or principles in communion with one another. They are the Petrine profile, expressed by the popes, who continue the presence of Peter, and by the hierarchy; and the Marian profile, which is the presence of Mary throughout the centuries in the many and varied charisms, both old and new, which enrich and beautify the Church with religious families, with ecclesial movements and new communities.

This Marian profile reminds us that the Church is built not only on the apostles, but also on the prophets and is made manifest in the charismatic aspect, the aspect that is prophetic, spiritual, that concerns holiness, an aspect which has always been found in the Church, and is still found today.

For von Balthasar, the Petrine, hierarchical principle is linked to the external structures of the Church, to the objective holiness found in the scriptures, the

---

44. John Paul II, Message to the world congress of ecclesial movements, 27 May 1998.

sacraments, the ministries, and also includes other elements, like canon law. The Marian principle is found in the spirit of holiness found in Mary and lived out in a dynamic manner in all that leads to making the Church holy. The institutional structure is ordered towards this Marian profile, which, unlike the former, unlike the hierarchy, will last for all eternity.

3. Priests Who Are "Mary"

The Marian and Petrine profiles of the Church are not only co-essential but they permeate each other. In the 1960s Chiara wrote, "Mary, who was a lay person like us, shows the Church that the essence of Christianity is love, and that priests and bishops, before having that role, need to be true Christians, living crucifixes, like Jesus, who founded his Church on the cross." Thousands of priests around the world, inspired by this intuition, strive to base their ministerial priesthood on living out their baptismal priesthood, giving of themselves in imitation of Jesus crucified. This results in an authentic and integral lifestyle that bears much fruit.

Priests who are "mothers"

The following text summarizes the main points made in a talk entitled "The Priest Today, the Religious Today" given by Chiara on April 30, 1982, to 7000 priests, religious and seminarians in the Paul VI Hall in the Vatican.

From the introduction to the guidelines for priests and permanent deacons who are focolarini

[1990]

This spiritual journey, which is also called "the Way of Mary," will help the focolarini who are priests to live to the full, as a necessary and fruitful support to their ministerial priesthood, their royal priesthood, for which Mary is their model.

Jesus wants to live in his priests, not only because of the charism they received with their ordination, but also because of the love that can make them perfect ("I in them"—Jn 17: 23).

And, since the spirituality of unity brings to full potential the royal priesthood, besides the ministerial priesthood, the focolarino who is also a priest will be, so to speak, a priest-Mary, a priest-mother, not only because as minister of God he nourishes the divine life in the faithful, but also because he generates them by remaining always anchored to the cross.

Priests who are Christ

From an article published in the Italian Focolare magazine, Città Nuova

10 February 1970

Among the divine words spoken by Jesus, there is one that makes your head spin because you realize that it was pronounced by God and it makes you understand the greatness of being chosen. It is a paradoxical comparison, but true and rich in mystery. And Christ addresses himself to those who would be his priests throughout the centuries: "As the Father has sent me, so I send you" (Jn 20: 21).

Therefore, who is the priest?

It is the person Christ has chosen to continue his mission in time.

Unfortunately, sometimes the priest is not like that. And if the priest is not Christ, he is nothing. His sermons are empty and the churches deserted.

Because the word that Christ gave was himself.

If the priest first lives what he preaches and then speaks, his word will be Christ and he himself will be another Christ. His sermons will draw crowds of people and the churches will be full to overflowing.

Because it is not so much knowledge that makes a priest, but the charism invigorated by love. '

And so the work he does for the benefit of those entrusted to him has to be done by Christ in him.

And Christ in him will work miracles, obtain the impossible in prayer, illuminate his entire pastoral activity with wisdom, which will suggest thousands of new ways to bring, with the means available today, the eternal word of God to humanity.

And people require, now more than ever, authenticity. It is no longer enough to have people who happened to have been ordained as priests. We need priests who are Christ, priests who [offer themselves as] victims for humanity.

We need authentic Christs, always ready to die for everyone.

If this is the measure of love in the life of the priest, he need not be afraid of having nothing to do, nor worry about having to change his profession.

He will see the piece of Church entrusted to him become a garden, a garden with weeds, of course, with hatred, but also with the fruitful love that does not stop radiating at the edge of this garden, but goes well beyond.

It is like Ars [the town where St. John Vianney was pastor], yes, just like Ars. When their pastor gave himself totally for his people, after God of course, people came from far away to breathe in the atmosphere of Christ, to feed on him in order to live.

Let's face it, let's say it out loud: in order to live!

Because without Christ, without priests-Christ, the world today too, even with all its magnificent and extraordinary discoveries does not really live. It agonizes, it dies.

Christ alone is Life.

Priests as the Church today wants them to be

In the context of talks she was giving on Jesus in the Eucharist, Chiara reflected on liturgy and asked, in the light of experience, what it is that characterizes priests who live deeply the spirituality of unity. She concludes: "They are priests as the Church wants them today," totally one with the people of God.

1976

Love has led these priests to break down every barrier, no matter how slight, that divided them from their brothers and sisters, and so when they celebrate the Eucharist, either within the small family of the focolare household or in the big meetings (Mariapolises, congresses, various meetings) with thousands of people, they are already united with them in the name of Jesus, as is required. In the introduction to the new Italian Missal we read: "From the moment they meet, Christians from different places and environments must recognize that they are brothers and sisters. Christ present in their midst creates their unity. In fact, he said: 'Where two or three are gathered in my name, I am there among them' (Mt 18: 20)."

The rite is simple, as in a family. The Eucharist is not just the task of the priest, but of everyone. Those who have to read the various scripture passages prepare themselves, songs are chosen, including the entrance song which expresses the joy of the community assembled together. People make spontaneous offerings, and prayers of petition and thanksgiving. And the priest is there, at the center, to renew, in the name of Christ, the sacrifice of the cross. The strong presence of Jesus powerfully affects the hearts of the participants, and often people cannot hold back their tears, or they make very difficult resolutions, as if they were alone with Jesus on the altar. . . .

Then we receive communion in deep silence. . . .

And at the end, the assembly is invaded by a wave of joy, a witness to its unity with the risen Christ.

Then once the Eucharist is over, almost as an extension of it, priests and faithful take off! They bring love to others all day long, in homes and offices and meetings, where communion continues and brings liberation and the development of humankind in thousands of different circumstances all over the world. This is a duty, an obligation, if we want to go on loving as Christ loved.

This is the people of God that has become more fully of God, where the communion of goods takes place silently, but constantly and increasingly, serving thousands of needs; where communion with Christ grows through living his Word, and hearts are aflame with eagerness to evangelize.

These are our priests, completely one with the people of God, representatives of the people at the altar, vicars of Christ, the head of his body, Christ himself in the holy memorial.

Our priests are nothing other than priests! And what an extraordinary adventure that is!

4. Women and the Church's Marian Profile

In a meditation published in 1959, Chiara wrote, "When a woman is another Mary, which means virgin, mother and spouse, agony and paradise, but above all, 'one who gives God,' she can do much for everyone, because a woman, if she is truly a woman, is the heart of humanity." This was an intuition Chiara continued to develop throughout her life and in the Movement. At the time of the Second Vatican Council she wrote, "Besides launching a life of unity and spreading it everywhere, the Focolare has the task of giving a contribution to improving the place of women in the Church."

From a talk during a conference on "Mulieris dignitatem," [apostolic letter on the dignity of women] organized by the Catholic University and the Diocese of Spoleto.

Roccaporena, Italy, 1 June 1989

In the hierarchy of holiness, Mary, a woman, is the model of the Church

The pope brings out the original identity and vocation of women from the very depths of the Word of God. . . .

First the pope recalls the person of Mary, the mother of God, the Theotókos, and shows us the extraordinary dignity to which God elevates woman in her (see n 4-5). . . .

When it is a matter of carrying out the greatest work in history—the reconciliation and the reunification of all people with God and among them—God addresses himself to Mary and asks for her free consent so that the incarnation of the Son, the redeemer, may be accomplished in her. The pope then points out that the New Covenant "begins with a woman, *the* woman, in the annunciation at Nazareth." "This," he states, "is the absolute novelty of the Gospel." It is an indicative sign that in Christ "there is no longer male or female" (Gal 3: 28), that is that the reciprocal contraposition between man and woman is essentially overcome, because in him "all are one" (see n 11). . . .

In this way, the reality of love, the holiness to which, first and foremost, we are all called, and the royal priesthood that we must all live, are all being brought to the fore within the Church. And in the hierarchy of holiness, Mary, the "woman," is the "model" of the Church. She "precedes" us all. In her "the Church has already reached perfection" (see n. 7).[45]

---

45. See *Redemptoris Mater*

Woman can express the Marian profile

Woman, because of her singular relationship with Mary, is called in a particular way to be the reflection of love on earth, of intra-trinitarian love, to witness it and communicate it to the world. . . .

And by living love, especially mutual love, by "generating" Christ spiritually among people, women feel particularly close to Mary who gave Jesus physically to the world.

In every stage of life they can find their model in Mary, since she is the virgin, the fiancée, the spouse, the mother, the widow and, at the same time, open and interested in the vast problems of humanity, as is clear from the Magnificat.

Or, perhaps, it is Mary herself who, feeling that she has received from God the task to give back to women their dignity, as our times demand, models these women on herself. And above all, she teaches them what is the first secret of true Christian love: the cross, sacrifice. That is how Jesus, in a particular way, showed his love to the world. And that is how, Mary, participating in her son's passion, became the mother of all.

These women, following her, will have to take the same path as hers to become, in some way, the mothers of many. . . .

In this way, woman, living her vocation in full, with the faith, nobility and love of Mary, can reveal to the Church the "Marian dimension of the life of the disciples of Christ." She can keep alive and be the expression of the Marian profile of the Church of which, from time to time, the pope speaks and that he declares "equally—if not more—fundamental and characterizing . . . as the apostolic and Petrine profile."

There are, therefore, women who give real hope and are an example to many, because the Holy Spirit is at work in them. And who knows what surprises he still has in store for us. . .

The Church for the Third Millennium

In his message on the occasion of Chiara's death, Pope Benedict wrote: "There are many reasons to thank the Lord for the gift to the Church of this woman of great faith, a gentle messenger of hope and peace." He defined her as a "generous witness of Christ who gave herself unsparingly for the spread of the gospel message at every level of contemporary society, always attentive to the "signs of the times." In many ways, Chiara opened up new avenues for the people of God in an era marked by major challenges as well as by new opportunities.

1. In the "Global Village"

As Pope Francis has often said, we are living not in an "era of changes" but in a "change of era." In one of her last talks, an extract of which we publish here, Chiara speaks of the situation of the world today, in particular with reference to Europe, and yet what she says can also be applied to life throughout the world.

Between light and shadow, the birth of a new world

From a talk entitled, "What is the future for a multicultural, multi-ethnic and multi-religious society?"

Westminster Central Hall,
London, 19 June 2004

In recent years, our European societies have been affected by significant patterns of migration from east to west and from south to north. This phenomenon has had a profound impact on the composition of our continent, bringing to our cities an ever-greater diversity. Walking through the streets we see that mosques, for example, have been built and also many temples, in countries which, until a short while ago, were almost exclusively Christian.

At the same time, modern means of communication bring together individuals and peoples who are physically very distant from one another, so much so that the personal choices of a young person from the West might be profoundly influenced by what happens in Asia or in Africa. No one is foreign to us any longer because we "see" them, we know about them. Furthermore, economic and financial globalization has woven all our interests together, so that they are no longer separated from one another. Many current problems concern humanity as a whole, and no single nation can face them in isolation from the others. So we live in a world that has truly become, as people say, "a global village," a new and complex village. This situation opens up previously unheard-of opportunities for knowledge and development, even though fear, distrust and intolerance remain, especially because of the ever-present danger of terrorism.

A person who found himself in a situation in some ways similar to ours was Augustine of Hippo, a great saint and doctor of the Church. Faced with the fall of the Roman Empire because of the effect of the migration of peoples from the north and east, he had the grace and foresight to help Christians understand that the upheavals in their civilization which his contemporaries witnessed was not the end of their world, but the birth of a new world.[46] His was a vision that came from faith and from the conviction that God is not absent from history. God's love is such that it directs everything towards good. St. Paul himself said this: "We know that all things work together for good for those who love God" (Rom 8: 28).

And now—it seems to me—this same faith must sustain and guide us in our present-day situation.

2. "The Home and the School of Communion"

Right from the beginning of the Movement in the 1940s, Chiara prophetically observed, "In a world that is de-Christianized and materialistic, Christians will have to build a spiritual cloister, with Christ in their midst, wherever they are. If they are its pillars, then living water

---

46. See *The City of God*, but also the sermons in which St. Augustine speaks of the fall of Rome (n. 81, 105, 296 and 397).

will pour out of them for the good of many." As the third millennium approached, Chiara focused increasingly on the characteristics of a "spirituality of communion" that centers on Jesus living in the midst of people, a spirituality that renders his presence more visible. In 2001 Pope John Paul II affirmed: "To make the Church the home and the school of communion: that is the great challenge facing us in the millennium which is now beginning, if we wish to be faithful to God's plan and respond to the world's deepest yearnings." To achieve this goal, he pointed out, that "before making practical plans, we need to promote a spirituality of communion" (Novo millennio ineunte, *n. 43).*

Not only an "interior castle" but also an "exterior castle"

From her acceptance address when named "Author of the Year" by the Italian Catholic Union of Editors and Publishing Houses

Milan, 9 March 1995

In the two thousand years since the time of Christ, the Church has experienced, one after the other, the flowering of the most beautiful and fruitful spiritualities. Sometimes they occurred in the same period, adorning the spouse of Christ with many saints, like precious pearls and diamonds.

But in all this splendor one factor has always remained constant: spirituality was focused primarily on the advance of the individual towards God.

This was a consequence of the time when Christians lost the fervor of the first Jerusalem community, in which all were one heart and one soul. With the end of the persecutions, they sought to preserve their own personal faith by withdrawing into the desert, with the primary goal of keeping the first commandment, love of God. Those were the days of the hermits.

This development preserved many Christian ideals and produced many saints, but it did not put much emphasis on the place of one's neighbor in the spiritual life. In fact, one's neighbor was often considered to be an obstacle to a person's advance towards God. . . .

But times have changed. Now the Holy Spirit is inspiring people to walk together and to be of one heart and soul with all who share their convictions. . . .

Contemporary theologians foresaw a communitarian spirituality in our times and Vatican II proposed it. . . .

In our era the reality of communion is coming to the forefront. The kingdom of God is sought not just in individual persons, but in the midst of the people. . . .

In this way of unity, everything—our work, study and prayer, as well as our striving towards holiness or spreading the Christian life—takes on meaning and value, as long as we keep the presence of Jesus in our midst with our brothers and sisters, since that is the norm of norms for this way of life.

In this spirituality we reach holiness if we walk towards God in unity. . . .

St. Teresa of Avila, a doctor of the Church, speaks of the "interior castle," referring to the soul with the divine Majesty dwelling at its center, revealing and shedding light on everything in life, allowing the person to overcome every sort of trial. Even though St. Teresa drew all her daughters into this experience, it is a height of sanctity that is primarily personal.

But then came the moment, at least so it seemed to us, of discovery, of shedding light upon and building not just the "interior castle," but also "the exterior castle."

We see the whole Movement as an exterior castle, where Christ is present, illuminating every part of it, from the center to the periphery.

But if we consider that this new spirituality God is giving the Church today has reached leaders in the Church and in society, then we see that this charism creates an exterior castle not only of our Movement but tends to do so as well of the whole body of the Church and of society.

One in Christ: the first form of evangelization!

On February 16, 1995, Pope John Paul II received in audience a large group of bishop-friends of the Focolare Movement. In his talk to them he underlined the need to have a robust spirituality of communion at the basis of the life and mission of the Church. Chiara took up this theme in a telephone conference call with the communities of the Movement throughout the world.

23 March 1995

A group of seventy bishops, friends of our Movement, were recently received in an audience with the pope, who addressed them with a brief but very interesting talk. . . .

After expressing his joy in meeting this group of bishops . . . the pope affirmed that a collective or communitarian spirituality is "a constitutive aspect of the Christian vocation" (in other words, it belongs to the very nature of the Christian vocation), because, he says, "The Lord Jesus did not call the disciples to follow him individually, but in an inseparably personal and communitarian way." . . .

Further ahead, with the words used by the Council he defines the Church as an "icon of the holy Trinity, mystery of communion and sacrament of unity, so that the communion among the members of the Church is the primary and the principal sign she offers so that the world may believe in Christ.". . .

Because, he affirms, "to be one in Christ is the first and abiding form of evangelization carried out by the Christian community.". . .

John Paul II continues then by saying, "Our world today demands a new evangelization," which he feels is synonymous with "responding to this primordial personal and ecclesial (that is, communitarian) vocation: to form in Christ 'one heart and soul' (Acts 4: 32).". . .

Therefore, he says: "a renewed proclamation of the gospel cannot be consistent and effective if it is not accompanied by a sound spirituality of communion. . . ."

3. Ecumenical Prophecy

At an ecumenical meeting of bishop-friends of the Focolare, during an ecumenical prayer service in St. Anne's Evangelical Lutheran church in Augsburg, Chiara commented: "If we want the civilization of love, which the third millennium seems to expect of us, nothing is more urgent than generating a strong current of love in the world." She didn't realize then that the Joint Declaration on the Doctrine of Justification would be signed in that very church one year later, on October 31, 1999.

To form one single Christian people

Though there is not yet full communion among the Churches, the commitment to live mutual love among Christians of various Churches is already forming a portion of Christianity that is living the experience of being one heart and one soul.

St. Anne's Church, Augsburg
29 November 1998

If we Christians take a fresh look at our history over the past two thousand years, and in particular at the second millennium, we cannot help but be saddened to see that it has often been characterized by a series of conflicts, disputes and mutual incomprehension.

Certainly, all these things were caused by circumstances—historical, cultural, political, geographical, and social circumstances. But they also happened because among Christians there was a lack of what should have been their specific unifying feature, which is <u>love</u>.

And so today, as we seek to put right all that went so seriously wrong, we need to focus our attention on the source of our common faith, on God who is Love, and because he is Love, calls us to love as well. . . .

In the light of God who is Love

In these times it seems to me that it is really him, God-Love, who, in a certain way, must return and reveal himself anew not only to the heart of each of us Christians, but also to the churches that we compose. God loves the churches for the times when throughout history they have acted according to the design that he had for them. But also—and here we see the wonder of God's mercy—he loves them even for the times when, because Christians became divided from one another, they did not correspond to his design, provided that now they seek full communion with the other churches.

It is this deeply consoling conviction that made Pope John Paul II, trusting in the one who brings good from evil, give the following answer, when he was asked, "Why would the Holy Spirit have permitted so many different divisions?" While recognizing that it could have been because of our sins, he added: "Could it not be that these divisions have also been . . . a path continually leading the Church to discover the untold wealth contained in Christ's Gospel and in the redemption accomplished by Christ? Perhaps all this wealth would not have come to light otherwise. . ."[47]

Therefore, we must believe in God, who is Love for us and for the churches.

Mutual love between the churches

But, if God loves us, we cannot remain inactive before such divine goodness. As true children we must return his love also as churches.

During the centuries each church has, to a degree, become set in its ways, because of the waves of indifference, lack of understanding and even of mutual hatred.

---

47. John Paul II, *Crossing the Threshold of Hope* (New York: Knopf, 1995), 152-153.

What is needed in each church is a supplement of love. So, we need love for each other's churches, and mutual love among the churches. We need the love that leads each church to be a gift for the others, so that we can foresee in the Church of the future that there will be just one truth, but that it will be expressed in different ways, seen from different viewpoints, made more beautiful by the variety of interpretations.

Jesus forsaken, the bright star for the ecumenical journey

Mutual love, however, is truly evangelical, and therefore valid, only if it is practiced in the measure desired by Jesus. He said: "Love one another as I have loved you. No one has greater love than this, to lay down one's life for one's friends" (Jn 15: 12-13). And Jesus gave his life for us, in his passion and death, when he suffered during the agony in the garden, when he was scourged, and crowned with thorns, and when he was crucified, but he also suffered in that climax of his agony, expressed in the cry: "My God, my God, why have you forsaken me?" (Mt 27: 46). . . .

But if this is so, it is not difficult to see in him, in Jesus forsaken, the brightest star which should throw light on our ecumenical journey.

It seems that efforts in the field of ecumenism will be fruitful in so far as those who dedicate themselves to it, see in Jesus crucified and forsaken, who re-abandons himself to the Father, the key to understanding every disunity and to re-establishing unity; who find in him the light and the strength not to stop in the traumas and in the cracks of division, but always to go beyond and find a solution, all possible solutions.

Jesus among Christians of different churches

Mutual love leads then to achieving unity. When unity is lived it has an effect, and this too is a key point for a living ecumenism. It brings about the presence of Jesus among people, in the community, gathered in his name. He said, "Where two or three are gathered in my name, I am there among them" (Mt 18: 20). Jesus in the midst between a Catholic and a Lutheran who love one another, between Anglicans and Orthodox, between an Armenian and a member of the Reformed Church! How much peace this would bring even now, how much light it would shed on a productive ecumenical journey.

Moreover, this presence of Jesus is a gift which also lessens the pain of waiting for the day when we will all share together his presence in the Eucharist.

We also need to have great love for the Holy Spirit, who is the personification of Love, who binds in unity the Persons of the blessed Trinity and is the bond between the members of the mystical body of Christ.

I know, also from experience, that if we all live in this way, there will be exceptional fruits. There will be one effect above all. By living together these different aspects of our Christianity, we will realize that we form, so to speak, one Christian people, that can be a leaven to help bring full communion among the churches.

4. A Respectful Proclamation

During a trip to India, Chiara observed how the Church exists "also outside of it." By way of confirmation, she cited Thomas Aquinas who affirmed that the Church extends to all those for whom Jesus died, thus to all humankind. Through dialogue, Chiara states, the Church opens to "herself outside of herself and present in the seeds of the Word." On this basis we can have a "respectful proclamation" that unites evangelization with sincere dialogue.

Dialogue: a totally modern word

From a talk, "What is the future for a multicultural, multi-ethnic and multi-religious society?"

London, 19 June 2004

Ready to learn from everyone

It is a matter of weeping with those who weep, rejoicing with those who rejoice. Making ourselves one: this is the attitude that guided the apostle Paul, who wrote that he made himself a Jew with the Jews, Greek with the Greeks, all things to all people (see 1 Cor 9: 19-22). It is most important that we follow his example so that we can establish a sincere, friendly dialogue with everyone.

Yes, dialogue. It is a totally modern word. Dialogue means that people meet together and even though they have different ideas, they can speak calmly and with sincere love to their partner in dialogue, seeking to find some kind of agreement that can clarify misunderstandings, resolve disputes and conflicts and even at times eliminate hatred. This dialogue, especially among the faithful of different religions, is necessary and indispensable today more than ever if we want to avert the great evils threatening our societies.

It has been written: "To know the other person's religion implies putting yourself in the shoes of the other, seeing the world as he or she sees it, grasping what it means for the other to be Buddhist, Muslim, Hindu. . ."[48] This is not easy. It demands complete emptiness of self, that we put aside the ideas in our mind, the affections in our heart, all that is our own will, so as to identify with the other person.

It is a matter of putting aside, for the moment, even what is most important and most precious to us: our own faith, our own convictions, in order to be "nothing" in front of the other person, a "nothingness of love." In this way we put ourselves in an attitude of learning, and there is always something to learn.

If we are motivated by this kind of love, the other person will be able to express him or herself because they see in us someone who accepts them. They can give themselves because they find in us someone who listens. We come, then, to know their faith, their culture, their terminology. We enter their world, we become inculturated in some way in it and are enriched. Having this attitude, we contribute to making our multicultural societies become intercultural—that is, composed of cultures that are open to one another and in a profound dialogue of love with each other.

---

48. Frank Whaling, *Christian Theology and World Religions: A Global Approach* (Baskingstoke UK: Marshall Pickering, 1986), 130-131.

Made brothers and sisters by truth

Our complete openness and acceptance, then, predisposes the other person to listen to us. We have noticed that when someone dies to him or herself in order to "make themselves one" with others, the others are struck by this and often ask for an explanation.

Then we can move on to what the pope calls "respectful announcement." "Respect" is the key word in every dialogue. So as to be true to God and to ourselves, and to be sincere with our neighbor, we share what our faith affirms on the subject we are talking about, without imposing anything on the other person, without any trace of proselytism, but only out of love.

However, through the Holy Spirit who is always present when we love, our brothers or sisters are struck by something we say, something "alive," in a supernatural sense, re-awakening in their hearts. These are the "seeds of the Word" that the Second Vatican Council spoke of, which the love of God has placed in every religion.

While we are speaking, our brothers or sisters come to appreciate some aspect of those purely human values, found also in people who profess no religious faith, values that the Lord, in creating us, planted in every person and in every culture.

And on the basis of these "seeds," or values, we can offer—always as a service—with gentle and boundless discretion, those aspects of truth we possess which can give greater fullness and completeness to what our neighbor already believes. Thus it is that, first, the other person has given to us and then we do the same. In the atmosphere of communion created by this exchange of gifts the truth is gradually revealed and we feel that it has brought us closer to one another, as brothers and sisters.

5. Together for Peace and Fraternity

If the ultimate goal of the Church is for everyone to reach the heavenly homeland, the people of God is called to be within humanity a catalyst of justice and sharing, of fraternity and peace, while journeying towards "the new heavens and new earth."

What is impossible for millions who are isolated

From a talk, "What is the future for a multicultural, multi-ethnic and multi-religious society?"

London, 19 June 2004

Real, true and heartfelt fraternity is the fruit of a love capable of making itself dialogue, relationship, a love which, far from arrogantly closing itself within its own confines, knows how to open up to others and work together with all people of good will in order to build unity and peace in the world. . . .

We know that the causes of terrorism are many, but one of them, the deepest, is the unbearable suffering of a world divided between one fifth who are rich and four fifths who are poor. This has generated and continues to generate smoldering resentments in people and causes outbreaks of violence and revenge.

More equality is needed, more solidarity, above all a more equal sharing of goods.

However, as we know, goods do not move by themselves, they cannot walk on their own. People's hearts must be touched and moved, they must be open to one another.

To this end we need to spread among as many people as possible the idea and practice of fraternity, and—given the enormity of the problem—the idea and practice of a universal fraternity. Brothers and sisters know how to look after one another, they know how to help one another, how to share what they have.

A decisive contribution by religions

To meet this unprecedented challenge, the contribution of religions is decisive.

Where else, if not in the great religious traditions, could a strategy of fraternity begin, a strategy that could bring about real change even in international relations? . . .

We know from experience that anyone who wants to move the mountains of hatred and violence in today's world faces an enormous task. But what is impossible to millions of divided and isolated individuals seems to become possible for those who have made mutual love, mutual understanding and unity the driving force of their lives. . . .

Then the day when mutual love will blossom also among peoples will not be far off.

Is it a hopeless dream? No, it is God's most heartfelt desire, it is Jesus' last testament, his prayer for unity, and it will become a reality. If he, who is the Son of God, asked the Father for the unity of all, this prayer will surely be granted.

For Further Reading

Ciardi, Fabio. *Koinonia*. London: New City, 2017.

Lubich, Chiara. A New Way. New York: New City Press, 2002.

———. *The Cry*. New York: New City Press, 2001.

———. *Diary 1964/65*. New York: New City Press, 1987.

———. *Early Letters*. New York: New City Press, 2012.

———. *Essential Writings*. New York: New City Press, 2007.

———. *Fragments of Wisdom*. Bombay: Mariapolis Trust, 1992.

———. *Knowing How to Lose*, Revised Edition. London: New City, 2015.

———. *The Living Presence*. London: New City, 1996.

———. *Man's Yes to God*. London: New City, 1982.

———. *Manifesto*. London: New City, 1975.

———. *Mary, Flower of Humanity* London: New City, 2017.

———. *Mary: Her Identity, Our Identity*. New York: New City Press, 2018.

———. *May They All Be One*. New York: New City Press, 2016.

———. *Servants of All*. New York: New City Press, 1978.

———. *Yes, Yes, No, No*. London: New City, 1977.

About Chiara Lubich

Chiara Lubich (1920-2008) was founder of the Focolare Movement (The Work of Mary). Born in Trent, Italy, her baptismal name was Silvia. In 1943, when she entered the Third Franciscan Order, she took the name Chiara because she was attracted by St. Clare of Assisi's radical choice of God. 1943 also marks the year that Chiara Lubich made a vow of chastity, and it has become the year associated with the birth of the Focolare. In the course of her life, she saw the spirituality of the Focolare—the spirituality of unity—grow around the world. She was awarded 15 honorary doctoral degrees, numerous civic awards, the Templeton Prize for Progress of Religion, and the UNESCO Peace Prize. She published more than 50 books in 29 languages.

Today, the Focolare Movement that she founded is present in 182 countries. It has approximately 2 million adherents and people who are sympathetic to its goals—the majority being Roman Catholic. There is a growing number of non-Catholics from 350 churches and ecclesial communities. The Movement also includes many from other world faiths, for example, Jews, Muslims, Buddhists, Hindus and Sikhs. Then there are also those in the Movement who do not adhere to any particular religious faith.

NCP

New City Press

New City Press is one of more than 20 publishing houses sponsored by the Focolare, a movement founded by Chiara Lubich to help bring about the realization of Jesus' prayer: "That all may be one" (John 17:21). In view of that goal, New City Press publishes books and resources that enrich the lives of people and help all to strive toward the unity of the entire human family. We are a member of the Association of Catholic Publishers.

www.newcitypress.com
202 Comforter Blvd.
Hyde Park, New York

Periodicals
Living City Magazine
www.livingcitymagazine.com

Scan to join our mailing list
for discounts and promotions
or go to
www.newcitypress.com
and click on
"join our email list."